How the Book of James Teaches Us To Be True Disciples of Jesus

Dyron Daughrity

PUBLICATIONS

An Imprint of Sulis International Press
Los Angeles | Dallas | London

HOW THE BOOK OF JAMES TEACHES US TO BE TRUE DISCIPLES OF JESUS

Copyright ©2023 by Dyron Daughrity. All rights reserved.

Except for brief quotations for reviews, no part of this book may be reproduced in any form or by any electronic or mechanical means, including information storage and retrieval systems, without written permission from the publisher. Email: info@sulisinternational.com.

Cover design by Sulis International Press.
Front cover photo by Elianna Gill.
Back cover photo by Jon Tyson.

ISBN (print): 978-1-958139-30-1
ISBN (eBook): 978-1-958139-31-8

Published by Keledei Publications
An Imprint of Sulis International
Los Angeles | Dallas | London

www.sulisinternational.com

Contents

1. How to Live Like a True Disciple of Jesus 1
2. The Way of Stability 13
3. Don't Be Deceived 23
4. Do What It Says 33
5. The Streets of Philadelphia 43
6. Well-Done is Better Than Well-Said 51
7. Taming the Tongue 61
8. Don't Become God's Enemy 71
9. The Wealthy Elephant in the Room 81
10. Patience Means Firmness of Faith 93
11. Prayer, Confession, and Healing 103
12. Reflecting Back on Our Study of James 113
About the Author 121
About the Publisher 123

1. How to Live Like a True Disciple of Jesus

Epistle of Straw?

The book of James may have been the first book of the New Testament that was written down. Obviously, the *events* of the gospels are older, but they likely weren't completed until years *after* James was written. It is an old letter that the early Christians considered to be authentic and authoritative. We would do well to study it. Its words are from the brother of Jesus. Since James was considered an authority in the early church in Jerusalem, his letter has survived the test of time, and has become one of the stalwart texts of the New Testament.

Unfortunately, a few Protestants have some ambivalence when it comes to the book of James, since Martin Luther–the founder of Protestantism–considered James an "epistle of straw." He did not like its central teaching, that "faith without works is dead" (James 2:26). Luther was all about grace. He often proclaimed "sola fide," or, "faith alone." What he meant was that we are saved by faith alone. Luther loved Ephesians 2:8,

> "For it is by grace you have been saved, through faith—and this is not from yourselves, it is the gift of God—not by works, so that no one can boast."

This first chapter is entitled "How to Live like a True Disciple of Jesus." It is a bit of an introduction to James, and will hopefully serve as a helpful and concise orientation to this wonderful little book. I hope you will come to love James as much as I have. But, more importantly, I hope this study will equip you to be more obedient—and effective—in your walk with Christ.

Half-Brother?

Following Jesus is not easy, as James is going to make clear to us. In the natural, we are sinners. We tend to have hearts that want to rebel. That want to have our own way. That yearn for things that are not godly. James comes across as pretty strict in his teaching.

But you will notice that James's teachings echo the teachings of Jesus. This happens a lot in James. And it makes perfect sense, since James was the half-brother of our Lord. He definitely shared Jesus's thought world, his verbal expressions, probably even some of Jesus's facial expressions. They were brothers. They grew up together. They were in the same rooms at the same time during most of their growing up years. What a thought! James was a fortunate man to get to grow up next to the Son of God as ... his half-brother.

Half-brother? That's right. They shared the same mother, but not the same father. Jesus was conceived by the Holy Spirit. James was conceived by Joseph.

James was probably the second oldest boy in the family. There were at least 7 children born to Mary, according to Matthew 13:55-56. That text tells us that Jesus's brothers were James, Joseph, Simon, and Judas. Then it mentions there were *sisters* (plural). Thus, we encounter at least six siblings in that text, and—with Jesus—it makes at least 7 children born to Mary. Mary likely had some children that did not live beyond infancy, as that was common in the first century A.D.

We don't know how many sisters Jesus had, since women were often not named in antiquity. And they were not named in that text. In a patriarchal society, it was common for the men to be listed by name—usually oldest to youngest. However, women were usually referred to in the plural as *women* or *sisters*.

Jesus and James were raised together, in Nazareth, as well as in the general Galilee region of Israel. They sat at the table together, played together, attended synagogue together, worked with their father together, and studied the Torah together. We can say with some confidence that the book of James is probably more similar to the literal teachings of Jesus than any other book in the New Testament. They thought alike. They knew each other in a way that nobody else could have. They were brothers.

An Esteemed Pillar

There is quite a bit of information on James in the New Testament. First, we know him as the author of this epistle. Like most of the other General Epistles—which include Hebrews, 1 and 2 Peter, 1, 2, 3 John, and Jude—the Book of James takes its title from the author. James was a common name in New Testament times. In fact, there are four individuals named James in the New Testament, but scholars are united in the view that this epistle was written by the brother of Jesus.

In 1 Corinthians 15:3-8 we learn that Jesus appeared to James—personally—after he resurrected, which made a huge impact on James, as he did not believe in the Lordship of Jesus until *after* this incident.

For what I received I passed on to you as of first importance: that Christ died for our sins according to the Scriptures, that he was buried, that he was raised on the third day according to the Scriptures, and that he appeared to Cephas, and then to the Twelve. After that, he appeared to more than five hundred of the brothers and sisters at the same time, most of whom are still living, though some have fallen asleep. *Then he appeared to James*, then to all the apostles, and last of all, he appeared to me also, as to one abnormally born.

The biblical text also reveals that James and the other brothers did not believe in Jesus during his earthly ministry. This is found in John 7:1-5,

After this, Jesus went around in Galilee. He did not want to go about in Judea because the Jewish leaders there were looking for a way to kill him. But when the Jewish Festival of Tabernacles was near, Jesus' brothers said to him, "Leave Galilee and go to Judea, so that your disciples there may see the works you do. No one who wants to become a public figure acts in secret. Since you are doing these things, show yourself to the world." *For even his own brothers did not believe in him.*

Galatians 1:19 reveals that, once James became a believer, he was accepted as a very close associate of the apostles. In fact, he seems to be the leader of the Jerusalem church, according to several places in the New Testament (Acts 12:17, 15:13, 21:18, and Galatians 2:12). In Galatians 2:9, Paul refers to James, Peter, and John as the "esteemed pillars" of the early church. That's a big compliment, especially coming from Paul. In fact, Paul tells us that it was these three men who legitimized *his own* ministry among the Gentiles. In a wonderful passage–Galatians 2:8-10–Paul writes the following:

For God, who was at work in Peter as an apostle to the circumcised, was also at work in me as an apostle to the Gentiles. James, Cephas (Peter), and John, those *esteemed pillars*, gave me and Barnabas the right hand of fellowship when they recognized the grace given to me. They agreed that we should go to the Gentiles, and they to the circumcised. All they asked was that we should continue to *remember the poor*, the very thing I had been eager to do all along.

This passage from Galatians 2 sheds some important light on James and his familiarity with his brother's teaching. James taught things very similar to what Jesus taught.

We see in the ministry of Jesus a strong concern for the poor. A *privileging* of the poor, if you will. And we also see a tendency to warn the rich, even rebuke them at times, if they began to *serve* money, or, as Jesus calls it, "mammon."

James has that very same attitude, evinced not only in the book of James, but also in this Galatians 2 text by Paul. Paul tells us that James, Peter, and John legitimized and authorized his ministry among the Gentiles, as long as he and Barnabas continued to "remember the poor." Of course, Paul tells us that this is precisely what he had meant to do all along.

Early Christianity–Jesus, James, Paul–they all seemed very concerned about poor people. I suppose those of us who follow Jesus should be thinking more about the poor as well. It seems to be a fundamental concern of the early "pillars of the church."

The Search for the Historical James

Not only is James a major figure in the Bible, he was also known *outside* of the New Testament witness, by the Jewish historian Josephus, who actually worked as a historian for the Roman government. Josephus lets us know when James was martyred—it was in the year A.D. 61 or 62. We also learn from Josephus that James and some other Christians were stoned to death on account of breaking Jewish laws. It is recorded in Josephus's *Antiquities of the Jews* 20:9:1,

> But this younger Ananus, who, as we have told you already, took the High Priesthood, was a bold man in his temper, and very insolent. He was also of the sect of the Sadducees: who are very rigid in judging offenders above all the rest of the Jews: as we have already observed. When therefore Ananus was of this disposition, he thought he had now a proper opportunity [to exercise his authority]. Festus was now dead; and Albinus was but upon the road. So he assembled the Sanhedrim of judges, and brought before them the brother of Jesus who was called Christ, whose name was James: and some others; [or, some of his companions.] And when he had formed an accusation against them as breakers of the law, he delivered them to be stoned. But as for those who seemed the most equitable of the citi-

zens, and such as were the most uneasy at the breach of the laws, they disliked what was done.[1]

Early church history tells us that James was known as "James the Just" because of his righteousness and outstanding virtue.[2] We are told that he was elected by the early Christians to lead the Jerusalem church. It is said that James refused to drink alcohol, and was a vegetarian. He may have taken the biblical "Nazarite Vow" (Numbers 6:1-21) because he did not allow his hair to be cut, nor did he anoint himself with oil, or even bathe.[3] He was known by the early church fathers as "Camel Knees" because he prayed so often that he developed calluses and corns on his knees, making them knobby.[4]

As mentioned earlier, for a New Testament book, James is old. His epistle can be reliably dated to the mid- to late A.D. 40s, "making it the earliest written book of the New Testament canon."[5]

---

[1] This translation of Josephus is from the University Chicago, located at: http://penelope.uchicago.edu/josephus/ant-20.html.

[2] This is from Eusebius, who quotes Hegesippus.

[3] The vow is described in Numbers 6. For James being associated with the vow, see Acts 21:17-26. Hegesippus (A.D. 110–180) is the source that tells us much information about James the Just.

[4] Eusebius, quoting Hegesippus, "He alone, I say, was wont to go into the temple; and he used to be found kneeling on his knees, begging forgiveness for the people, so that the skin of his knees became horny like that of a camel's, by reason of his constantly bending the knee in adoration to God, and begging forgiveness for the people." See: https://nazarenejudaism.com/?page_id=176.

[5] John Macarthur, *James*, p. 1.

The Jerusalem Council

We see the authority of James on display in Acts 15, in what is called "the Jerusalem Council." This was the first council of Christianity, and it was supremely important. The Jerusalem Council–which occurred around A.D. 50–was crucial for establishing what Gentiles had to do in order to join the Jesus movement, known at that time as "the Way." At this council, we see Christianity clearly moving from a Jewish thing to a (mainly) Gentile thing.

The Jesus followers were happy that Gentiles were coming into the faith, but it provoked many questions. Jews were pretty insular in their understanding of religion. There were Jews and there were Gentiles (non-Jews). It was a pretty basic understanding of the world's people: us (Jews) and them (Gentiles).

At that council in Acts 15, we see Peter and James stand up and take the leading roles among the early church leaders. Peter tells everyone that God had done a new thing: He had given His Holy Spirit to non-Jews–if they have faith in Christ. People are saved by the "grace of the Lord Jesus," according to Peter's sermon in Acts 15, verse 11.

Then we witness James's leadership in the Jerusalem Council. He speaks with authority about how God had chosen Gentiles to be His people. He quotes from the prophet Amos, letting them know that Gentiles should be accepted. They don't have to become Jews first. When they become believers in Christ, they don't have to legalistically follow every single rule found in the Torah–the first five books of the Bible known as the Five Books of Moses.

But at that council in Acts 15, James lists four things the new Gentile converts to Christianity should do:

1. they must not eat food polluted by idol worship;

2. they must abstain from sexual immorality as defined by Judaism;

3. they must not eat meat from a strangled animal (presumably due to the inhumane handling of the animal); and

4. they must not drink blood.

This list of prohibitions might seem odd, but early Gentile Christians needed to honor these dietary laws, or else they would gravely offend the Jews in their midst. In other words, these teachings were necessary for table fellowship, which was then and still is crucial for Christianity. Table fellowship was at the heart of early Christianity, as displayed in the early Christian Love Feasts (known as "agape"), as well as in the Lord's Supper.

Another important idea from the Torah that emerges at the Jerusalem Council is sexual immorality. Gentiles had an extremely different understanding of sexuality in the Greco-Roman world. They permitted all sorts of sex acts and relations that Jews did not. And James reminds them that they absolutely must conform to the Jewish, Torah understanding of sexuality if they were to join the community of Jesus Christ. The Jewish understanding of sexual relations, and prohibitions, is listed in Leviticus chapter 18. It is an extensive list of prohibitions, so Gentiles would have been required to familiarize themselves with that list, and to honor it if they were to join the early Christian movement.

The Proverbs of the New Testament

When we read the book of James, we are transported back to some of the earliest Christian debates and discussions. It is similar to what we encounter in some of Paul's writings, especially in the Corinthian letters. We enter into another culture, far different from our own in many ways, but very similar in others.

In James, we hear an authoritative voice, a blood brother to Jesus, and a crucial position of leadership in the Jerusalem church. We must remember that Jerusalem was ground zero for the Christian faith. It was where Christianity began. It was the mother church. Jesus died and resurrected there. When you go to Jerusalem, even today, you feel that you are in a very special place. It is where Christianity—now the world's largest faith—began.

Bethlehem is wonderful. Nazareth is fascinating. The Sea of Galilee is incredible. But Jerusalem is special. It was the epicenter of the early church. And James was the leader there in the early days of the faith. His voice is crucial.

In James, we encounter some of the most memorable phrases in all of the Bible. Some scholars refer to James as the Proverbs of the New Testament. His is so quotable, succinct, and powerful. Here are but a few of the nuggets of wisdom we find in James:

- The testing of your faith produces perseverance (1:3).

- If any of you

- wisdom, you should ask God (1:5).

- Every good and perfect gift is from above (1:17).

- Everyone should be quick to listen, slow to speak, and slow to become angry (1:19).

- Do not merely listen to the Word, and so deceive yourselves. Do what it says (1:22).

- Whoever keeps the whole law and yet stumbles at just one point is guilty of breaking all of it (2:10).

- Mercy triumphs over judgment (2:13).

- Faith by itself, if it is not accompanied by action, is dead (2:17).

- A person is considered righteous by what they do and not by faith alone (2:24).

- Not many of you should become teachers ... because you know that we who teach will be judged more strictly (3:1).

- No human being can tame the tongue; it is a restless evil, full of deadly poison (3:8).

- Where you have envy and selfish ambition, there you find disorder and every evil practice (3:16).

- You do not have because you do not ask God (4:2).

- Anyone who chooses to be a friend of the world becomes an enemy of God (4:4).

- God opposes the proud, but shows favor to the humble (4:6).

- Resist the devil, and he will flee from you (4:7).

- Humble yourselves before the Lord, and He will lift you up (4:10).

- What is your life? You are a mist that appears for a little while and then vanishes (4:14).

- If anyone knows the good they ought to do and doesn't do it, it is sin for them (4:17).

- Don't grumble against one another ... or you will be judged. The judge is standing at the door (5:9).

- Do not swear—not by heaven or by earth or by anything else. All you need to say is a simple "Yes" or "No." Otherwise, you will be condemned (5:12).

- If anyone among you is sick, let them call the elders of the church to pray over them and anoint them with oil in the name of the Lord (5:14).

- The prayer of a righteous person is powerful and effective (5:16).

What a collection of wisdom! These texts are but the tip of the iceberg as you enter into your study. There are many more to come.

In order to absorb the book of James most effectively, it will be important to read the book of James entirely and frequently during your study of this important and truly helpful text. If you allow the teachings of James into your heart, then you will be well on your way to becoming a more faithful and committed disciple of Jesus—just as James was.

2. The Way of Stability

James 1:1-11

James, a bondservant of God and of the Lord Jesus Christ,

To the twelve tribes which are scattered abroad:

Greetings.

2 My brethren, count it all joy when you fall into various trials, 3 knowing that the testing of your faith produces patience. 4 But let patience have its perfect work, that you may be perfect and complete, lacking nothing. 5 If any of you lacks wisdom, let him ask of God, who gives to all liberally and without reproach, and it will be given to him. 6 But let him ask in faith, with no doubting, for he who doubts is like a wave of the sea driven and tossed by the wind. 7 For let not that man suppose that he will receive anything from the Lord; 8 he is a double-minded man, unstable in all his ways.

9 Let the lowly brother glory in his exaltation, 10 but the rich in his humiliation be-

cause as a flower of the field he will pass
away. 11 For no sooner has the sun risen with a
burning heat than it withers the grass; its flower
falls, and its beautiful appearance perishes. So the
rich man also will fade away in his pursuits.

These are the opening words of the epistle of Jacob.

Jacob? Yes, that's right. The book that we call "James," is actually and literally titled "Jacobou Epistole," which means "Jacob Epistle."

During the Medieval Ages, the Greek name "Jacob" was changed to "James" in the English-speaking world. That's why when you are reading the "King James Version" of the Bible, you are actually reading the "King Jacob Version" of the Bible, as the English and Scottish Kings who were known as James actually took their names from the Hebrew Patriarch "Jacob." This is why, in your history classes, you probably had to study the "Jacobean" era of England, which came just after the Elizabethan era and just before the Caroline era (which was the era of Charles I).

Okay, enough of English history. Let's get back to Jacob ... which we now call James.

Today's lesson from James is found in James chapter 1, verses 1-11.

In today's text, we are going to receive two major lessons.

- The first one has to do with benefiting from our difficulties in life.

- The second one has to do with the perspective we should have when it comes to the rich and the poor people who are members of the church.

At the end of the lesson, I will provide a few "take homes" that we can implement into our personal lives.

James begins his epistle by calling himself a doulos, the Greek word for "slave" or "servant." James also specifically refers to Jesus Christ as his Lord here in chapter 1, verse 1. This is important because James only mentions Jesus Christ twice in his epistle, in 1:1 and 2:1. But it is clear in those two passages that James considers himself a mere servant, or slave, to Jesus.

James realizes that his own authority comes from Jesus. Jesus Christ is his master and his Lord. James only says what he is authorized by the Lord Jesus to say. So, this word here doulos, sometimes translated "bondservant," is crucial. It shows us where James knows he stands—he is a mere servant to the Master—who is Jesus Christ.

James knows His place, as did all of the apostles and early followers of Jesus. We all remember the famous saying by John the Baptist. When John saw Jesus, he pointed out that he is not even fit to untie the strap of Jesus's sandals (John 1:27). In another place, John the Baptist says, "Jesus must become greater, and I must become less" (John 3:30). That last statement should be on our walls, on our mirrors, and on the back windshields of our vehicles. Our purpose in life is to serve our Master, Jesus.

So, friends, we've just begun to study the Epistle of James, and the biggest takeaway so far is that James considered himself absolutely subservient to Jesus Christ. And just as it was for James, it should be for each one of us here.

After James introduces himself as a slave to God and to the Lord Jesus, he mentions his addressees: the tribes who are scattered abroad. The word used in Greek here is "diaspora." Many of us will know that word from the study of Jewish history. The diaspora refers to Jews who became scattered from the Assyrian invasion of Northern Israel in the 700s B.C., as well as the Jews in the Southern Kingdom who were scattered by the Babylonians in the late 500s B.C.

And that wasn't the end of the persecution. Many Christ-following Jews were on the run to escape local persecutions from people like Saul—before he was forced into submission by God and himself became a follower of Christ.

As we know, Saul's name was changed to Paul. It is easy to forget that early Christians went through major persecutions until Roman Emperor Constantine came onto the scene in the early A.D. 300s.

For about 300 years after the death of Jesus in A.D. 33 or so, Christianity was illegal. Following Jesus was illegal. Jesus himself was declared illegal—that's why he was killed. And his followers, like Peter, Paul, and James (and many others) were killed. They suffered. They were tracked. They were spied upon, and many of them were killed. This forms the background of the New Testament writings.

If we turn back to James, we can acknowledge that this letter was written by James to the diaspora—those Christians living in various places. James is functioning as a pastor to them.

Note that this letter is not written to a specific city—like Thessalonica, or Corinth, or Ephesus, or Rome. It is written to a general audience—wherever followers of Jesus might be.

James knew that the Christian community was suffering. Some of them would be killed soon. Some were on the run. James himself was stoned to death in A.D. 62—about 15 years after he wrote this epistle. There were threats and dangers in the air at this time. Christians were under surveillance.

James tells his beloved "brothers" (v. 2) to "count it all joy when you fall into various trials." I don't mean to minimize our challenges today, but few of us are on the cusp of a violent death, as these New Testament Christians were.

Nevertheless, let's apply James's words to our own context. What are your struggles?

- A deteriorating marriage?

- A squabble with family members over the estate of a deceased relative?

- A legal storm that you've been sucked into?

- A painful, headache-of-a-job that you don't enjoy at all?

- Perhaps you are spending more money than you are able to earn—and you know you will have to deal with the consequences at some point.

Friends, we all have struggles. James calls them trials. These are "tests of faith," and James tells us that we should—quite surprisingly—be joyful that we get to go through them.

I am reminded of Acts 5:40-42. You may remember the story. The apostles had just gotten out of prison. But almost immediately upon release, they got into big trouble for evangelizing again. So, they were called to appear before the religious court—the Sanhedrin. They had a quick trial. The religious authorities gave the apostles a physical beating. And then the members of the Sanhedrin Council told them never to evangelize again. And here's what happened next:

The apostles left the Sanhedrin, rejoicing because they had been counted worthy of suffering disgrace for the Name. Day after day, in the temple courts and from house to house, they never stopped teaching and proclaiming the good news that Jesus is the Messiah.

Just imagine. These guys were rejoicing that they were given the opportunity to suffer for Jesus.

And so should you. Like the apostles did, like James said, we should count it as something to be joyful about.

"Why?" you may ask? It seems crazy to be thankful for the trials in life. Here's why ... because you will become more mature. You will become more perfect in Christ. You will become strong and anchored and rooted.

I am reminded of the very first Psalm, Psalm 1:1-3,

> Blessed is the one
>   who does not walk in step with the wicked
> or stand in the way that sinners take
>   or sit in the company of mockers,
> 2 but whose delight is in the law of the Lord,
>   and who meditates on his law day and night.
> 3 That person is like a tree planted by streams of water,
>   which yields its fruit in season
> and whose leaf does not wither–
>   whatever they do prospers.

James is outlining for us the way.

Let us remember that early Christianity was known as "the Way" before it was known as Christianity. And James is outlining "the Way" for us in these verses.

And part of being on "the Way" is that we seek wisdom, by asking God.

- You aren't sure whether to move to a different city?

- You don't know whether to allow yourself to fall in love again?

- You don't know whether you should try to make amends with that family member who deeply hurt you?

According to James, the answer is this: Ask God for Wisdom. God will give it to you. I am reminded of the words of Jesus in Matthew 7:9-11,

> Which of you, if your son asks for bread, will give him a stone? Or if he asks for a fish, will give him a snake? If you, then, though you are evil, know how to give good gifts to your children, how much more will your Father in heaven give good gifts to those who ask him!

We have a trustworthy God who will give us wisdom to handle these difficult situations in life. But the key is that we ask with confidence. The key is that we trust that God will help us. We must not doubt. We must not have ambivalent hearts. James says,

If any of you lacks wisdom, let him ask of God, who gives to all liberally and without reproach, and it will be given to him. But let him ask in faith, with no doubting, for he who doubts is like a wave of the sea driven and tossed by the wind. For let not that man suppose that he will receive anything from the Lord; he is a double-minded man, unstable in all his ways.

Look with me at James 1:8. Let's look at that word "double-minded." The Greek word is *dipsucos*, which actually means "two souls."

And James has strong things to say to those who have a divided soul. Are you with God, or are you split on whether you're with him or not? James says that those who have a divided soul are "unstable."

You want stability in your marriage? Be committed to one person. You want to have effective prayers? Be committed to the one God, and not to other things. God must have your resolute commitment if you want to be firmly planted ... if you want to be stable.

The result of ambiguity in your Christian commitment will be instability, and you will also come up empty in your prayer life. James 1:7 says that divided souls "should not expect to receive anything from the Lord."

Friends, when you pray to God ... when you go to Him and ask Him for help ... when you ask Him for wisdom ... He wants to see a heart that is fully committed to him. Not half a heart. Don't go to God "half-heartedly."

Go to God with singular devotion. Go to Him with complete commitment. Go to your Father with one heart, one mind, and one soul that is fiercely devoted to Him and His will in your life.

And what does all of this have to do with the "testing of your faith?" What James 1:2-3 is saying is that your trials should make you more reliant upon God. Those trials will make you strong ... you will become more resolute in your commitments to the Lord. You will become patient and mature. You will stop being weak in your faith; rather, you will become strong and fit. Your prayers will become much more powerful and effective when you ask for things like wisdom.

Finally, in James 1:9-10, we get this section on rich and poor. Later in the book of James, we will encounter rich non-Christians. But in this section, we encounter rich Christians. We know they are Christians from the context of being "brothers and sisters" and fellows "believers" in verses 2 and 9.

James comes down hard on financial disparity in the church.

Why is James hard on rich folks here? Well, his half-brother (hint: that's Jesus) was, too.

Jesus said things like, "Truly I tell you, it is hard for someone who is rich to enter the kingdom of heaven. ... It is easier for a camel to go through the eye of a needle" (Matthew 19:23-24).

Similarly, the apostle Paul had some similar warnings. He writes in 1 Timothy 6:10, "The love of money is a root of all kinds of evil, for which some have strayed from the faith in their greediness, and pierced themselves through with many sorrows."

Several New Testament writers warn us that we must be careful with money. James pronounces approval on the poor of this world. Jesus does the same in the great Beatitudes (Matthew 5:1-12).

James tells the lowly folks to be proud of their humble circumstances. But he pronounces a warning to the rich—that they remain aware that life is quick. Your pursuits will eventually wither alongside your withering body. Your trophies will go into the trash. Your name will be forgotten. Eventually, all of your money will be spent by someone, possibly someone you never actually knew.

James 1:11 says, "The rich will fade away even while they go about their business."

Many of us see this play out in living color:

- A man dies at the end of his career without even spending his massive savings.

- A woman chases fame and fortune, only to be rejected and sent away in the end.

- You work so hard, chasing the promotion that never happens.

Let us remember ... it all belongs to God. Keep it all in perspective. Use your money to do meaningful things. Rich folks can bless the poor folks in the church. If wealthy folks have their priorities in order, they can be a huge blessing to those around them.

We've all known rich people who were extremely generous: blessed others, built churches, rescued someone in the church, offered extreme generosity. If James is speaking to you ... if you are wealthy ... then turn your wealth into blessings.

Let us not forget we are all dust. And to dust we will return.

Take-Homes from James 1:1-11

1. Like James, know your role. You are God's servant.

2. Pray hard for God's wisdom. But don't split your soul. Don't be a half-hearted Christian.

3. If you are one of the rich ones, then know you can't take it with you. Be a blessing. Use your money to bless people.

3. Don't Be Deceived

James 1:12-18

12 Blessed is the one who perseveres under trial because, having stood the test, that person will receive the crown of life that the Lord has promised to those who love him.

13 When tempted, no one should say, "God is tempting me." For God cannot be tempted by evil, nor does he tempt anyone; 14 but each person is tempted when they are dragged away by their own evil desire and enticed. 15 Then, after desire has conceived, it gives birth to sin; and sin, when it is full-grown, gives birth to death.

16 Don't be deceived, my dear brothers and sisters. 17 Every good and perfect gift is from above, coming down from the Father of the heavenly lights, who does not change like shifting shadows. 18 He chose to give us birth through the word of truth, that we might be a kind of first fruits of all he created.

In the second half of James chapter one, the author deals with some very personal things that each of us struggles with. James doesn't dance around the topic. Like he does throughout the entire book, he is going to put it out there. No holds barred.

What am I talking about?

James lays out for us the oldest story ever told about humans: that is, the story of temptation, sin, and death. You know, the story from Genesis.

Adam and Eve sinned. They regretted it and had shame. Due to their choice to sin, they were consigned to human death. However, in the end, God took care of them, and showed love and concern towards them. But the point of the Adam and Eve story is that we tend to sin when the most enticing bait is dangled in front of us.

In James 1:12-18, we are told that if we persevere during our trials ... if we withstand the tests and temptations ... then we will eventually "...receive the crown of life that the Lord has promised to those who love him." (v. 12)

Does that expression "crown of life" ring a bell? It probably does ring a bell in your mind because the book of Revelation says something very similar, in Revelation 2:10,

> Do not fear what you are about to suffer. Behold, the devil is about to throw some of you into prison, that you may be tested, and for ten days you will have tribulation. Be faithful unto death, and I will give you the crown of life.

Remember, in the last chapter, we talked about the context of early Christianity. It was frightening for the early Christians, as many of them were being killed on account of their commitment to Jesus Christ. The New Testament documents should be read with this context in mind.

I don't want to minimize our own trials and temptations, but let's recognize that these early Christians were deeply committed to their Lord and Savior, Jesus Christ. They had such strong faith. They knew that if they were killed in the persecution, then they would receive eternal life. They had no doubt that God was faithful. Their love for Christ exceeded their love for this life.

Then, in verse 13, James makes it crystal clear that God allows us to be tested, but God does not tempt us into sin. There is a crucial difference. God has always allowed his children to be tested. Think of Abraham. Think of Moses being tested by the Israelites. Think of Job being tested by his pain and suffering and horrific losses. Even Jesus was tested in the Garden. You'll remember this scene from Luke 22:42-43,

> Father, if you are willing, remove this cup from me. Nevertheless, not my will, but yours, be done." And there appeared to him an angel from heaven, strengthening him.

Jesus was put to the test. He wasn't required to go to the cross. But he faced his fears, saying: "Not my will, but yours be done."

Temptation is different from being tested. God does not tempt us, as James makes clear. We should never say that we are being tempted by God.

Rather, we ourselves get drawn to the bait out of our own "evil desires." The Greek words here are reminiscent of fishing, or of an animal being trapped by giving in to the temptation to bite the bait.

Much like Adam and Eve bit the forbidden fruit.

Friends, this passage here in James is a bit difficult to read. Verse 14 says, "Each person is tempted when they are dragged away by their own evil desire and enticed."

Each person. Each individual.

We are each drawn to our own individual selection of bait. Is it lust for money? Is it lust of the flesh? Is it addiction to that high that comes from those pills? Is it Jose Cuervo or Jack Daniels? Is it that delicious morsel of food after you've already eaten? Is it that desire to get revenge? "They will not get the last word, no sir!" Is it one more scroll on that social media page–that will take you deep into the late hours of the night?

What's your bait? I want you to think about this for a minute? James is talking to each one of us. As he says in verse 14, "Each person." That's you. That's me.

What's your bait? I have a little exercise for you. Ponder your bait. Think of it. And I want you to send an email to yourself right now. Write these words: "My bait is _____."

Why am I asking you to do this? Isn't this a bit personal? Isn't this a bit uncomfortable? Yes, it is. James meant it to be personal and uncomfortable. And I hope you'll return to this email this week, and just remind yourself of what your bait is.

Furthermore, James is pointing out something to us that we often don't think about when we start eyeing that bait. He says this in the next verse (v. 15): Then, after desire has conceived, it gives birth to sin. And sin, when it is full-grown, gives birth to death.

It reminds me of something the apostle Paul said in Romans 6:23, "For the wages of sin is death, but the gift of God is eternal life in Christ Jesus our Lord."

Yes, James is communicating something very similar to what Paul proclaims in Romans 6. Let's look at what Paul says in its full context (Romans 6:19b-23):

> Just as you used to offer yourselves as slaves to impurity and to ever-increasing wickedness, so now offer yourselves as slaves to righteousness leading to holiness.
>
> 20 When you were slaves to sin, you were free from the control of righteousness. 21 What benefit did you reap at that time from the things you are now ashamed of? Those things result in death!
>
> 22 But now that you have been set free from sin and have become slaves of God, the benefit you reap leads to holiness, and the result is eternal life. 23 For the wages of sin is death, but the gift of God is eternal life in Christ Jesus our Lord.

Friends, let us not blame others for our sins. We especially must not blame God, as some are prone to do, "I don't know why God did this to me." The truth is that we got ourselves into this fix. We got ourselves addicted. We saw the bait, and we stared at it. Like that fish destined for the frying pan, we swam around the bait for a while, considering whether we should take it. We thought long and hard about it. We considered the cost. And we took it anyway. We got hooked.

We were dragged away. We lusted, and we paid the price for that lust. We were *enticed*, as James says. And as some of us know, we allowed that sin to become a part of us. James uses the analogy of pregnancy. We conceive. We allow the sin into us. And the sin grows in us. And, in James's words, "...when sin is full-grown, it gives birth to death."

Some people are completely destroyed by their sin. The addiction completely overcomes their will, and they are unable to get free of it. A temptation can completely collapse a person's life. Destroyed relationships, broken families, careers cut short, happiness destroyed.

The apostle Paul wrestled mightily with sin, and he had the candor to tell us all about it in Romans 7:

> I am unspiritual, sold as a slave to sin. 15 I do not understand what I do. For what I want to do I do not do, but what I hate I do. 16 And if I do what I do not want to do, I agree that the law is good. 17 As it is, it is no longer I myself who do it, but it is sin living in me. 18 For I know that good itself does not dwell in me, that is, in my sinful nature. For I have the desire to do what is good, but I cannot carry it out. 19 For I do not do the good I want to do, but the evil I do not want to do—this I keep on doing. 20 Now if I do what I do not want to do, it is no longer I who do it, but it is sin living in me that does it.
>
> 21 So I find this law at work: Although I want to do good, evil is right there with me. 22 For in my inner being I delight in God's law; 23 but I see another law at work in me, waging war against the law of my mind and making me a prisoner of the law of sin at work within me. 24 What a wretched man I am! Who will rescue me from this body that is subject to death? 25 Thanks be to God, who delivers me through Jesus Christ, our Lord!

These are words many of us can relate to. We have this sin that seems to be so strong in us. We wrestle. We can't seem to beat it. But "Thanks be to God, who delivers us through Jesus Christ our Lord."

Let us just admit it right here: Where would we be without that sacrifice of Jesus on the cross? Where in the world would we be? I can't imagine where I'd be. As they say, "There but for the grace of God go I."

Then James gives us his advice in 1:16: "Don't be deceived, my dear brothers and sisters." Like Adam. Like Eve. Don't give into the tempter. Don't think you can rationalize your sin. Don't allow someone to draw you away from your convictions. Don't be deceived.

Know that if you take the bait, there will be consequences. Don't deceive yourself into thinking that you just might get away with it this time. As Jesus said in Luke 12:2,

> There is nothing concealed that will not be disclosed. There is nothing hidden that will not be made known. What you have said in the dark will be heard in the daylight, and what you have whispered in the ear in the inner rooms will be proclaimed from the rooftops."

Sin has the ability to make us deceive ourselves. We rationalize. We defend. We struggle to confess our sins because we deceive ourselves into thinking our sins are better kept in the dark.

James concludes this section of scripture with good news. He also goes back to referencing the Book of Genesis, when he refers to God as the Father of the heavenly lights in 1:17. "Let there be light!" was what God said in the earliest verses of the Bible. We serve a God of light, not a God of darkness. Our God is a good God. He gives us gifts. "Every good and perfect gift is from above," James says in 1:17. God is benevolent. He is not a shifty God who changes like the shadows. He is a rock. Our God is stable and solid.

And we are his ... *children*. As James says in 1:18, "God chose to give us birth through the word of truth." Just as God said, "Let there be light," and there was light, God also spoke us into existence. We are His first-fruits (1:18), meaning we are the children of the New Covenant. We as Christians are unique in God's creation. He called us, and we chose to follow Him. We are the children of the New Covenant, who put our faith in His Son. We are the first-fruits. We are the offering. We are His chosen people.

What James is doing here is letting us know that despite our sins, we have a God who calls us out of that mess. Our God is *faithful*. He will never leave us nor forsake us *despite our sins*.

God is not like the shifting shadows. I am reminded of that old hymn:

> There is no shadow of turning with Thee.
>
> God changes not, His compassions they fail not.
>
> As Thou hast been, Thou forever will be.
>
> Great is Thy faithfulness. Great is thy faithfulness.
>
> Morning by morning new mercies I see.
>
> All I have needed Thy hand hath provided.
>
> Great is Thy faithfulness, Lord, unto me.

Do you see what James does in this text? It's beautiful. He begins by telling us we are blessed if we withstand temptation, if we remain faithful amid testing. He tells us that if we can remain faithful, then we will receive the crown of life.

But then James takes us into the reality of sin, and what it can do to us. We can destroy ourselves. We must not blame others. We especially must not blame God for the chaos we create in our own lives because of our caving in to temptation. It is a sad situation. Some are carried away by their own sin, leading them into eternal death.

But then James reminds us that we have a good God, who is eager to give us gifts. He offers us a crown of eternal life. And His promises are true because His Word is solid. It isn't shifty like *human* promises tend to be.

Listen to James. His words are truth. His words may sting, but it's because they are true. And sometimes truth reveals things that need to be exposed. We have a God of light. In Him there is no darkness at all. Let us abandon our sin and guilt and turn our faces toward the "Father of the heavenly lights," as James calls Him (1:17).

Take-Homes from James 1:12-18

1. Know your bait. You will be tested, and you will face temptation. You can count on it. Be aware of your own vulnerabilities.

2. Be aware of the destruction that sin causes. There is no upside to sin. It leads to dark places. It leads to death.

3. Know that you are not alone in your temptations. God is with you in them. And you are not the first person to be tempted. Even Jesus was tempted. Yet he did not sin.

The "Good News," friends, is that your sin was dealt with on the cross. That is precisely what Christians openly acknowledge: "By His wounds we are healed."

4. Do What It Says

James 1:19-27

In this chapter, we encounter the most important lesson of the entire book of James. It is a kind of "thesis statement" for the epistle. This is not at all minimizing the importance of the other parts of the book. Rather, we could say all of the other parts of James *point* to this section.

The most crucial lesson of James chapter one—and in the entire Book of James—is that we *live out* our Christian faith.

Today's text puts us squarely in front of a mirror. I mean literally. James asks us to look into the mirror. But he doesn't want us to just *glance* into the mirror and then walk away. James wants us to settle down there, with the mirror in our hand, and just take a good, long, hard look. What kind of man are you? What kind of woman have you become? Are you the one who sees and forgets? Are you the one who allows God's teaching to go into one ear, and then it exits the other ear quickly? Are you the one who doesn't really think much about all of this?

James asks us to settle in and listen to the Word of God. James asks us if we are getting this whole Christianity thing right. James challenges us with pretty strong imperatives, such as his most famous instruction: "Do what it says" (James 1:22). This is the central phrase of the entire epistle.

If you are like me, you don't like to be talked to like this. You don't like someone to look you in the eye and say, "Obey."

Perhaps as Americans, we feel that our sense of individuality is more precious than our need to conform to anything that anybody tells us. This individualistic attitude is not wise. It is inherently pompous. When it comes to the Word of God, we are wise to "Do what it says."

Laws from the mouth of God will save your soul. They will give you eternal life. They will keep you from harm. They will keep you out of trouble. They will bless you, not harm you. They will build a hedge of protection around your life so that you will enjoy your days serving Jesus Christ, the Lord of all, the only-begotten Son of God, the authoritative Word from God to man.

James is not harsh here. Rather, he is expressing a message of love that comes directly from the mouth of God.

Please take a moment to ponder a crucial moment with Jesus—our Lord and our God—as he spoke with his inner circle, shortly before leaving this earth. These words are powerful, and I encourage you to ponder them very carefully as I read them now. They are from John 14:15-24:

> 15 "If you love me, keep my commands. 16 And I will ask the Father, and he will give you another advocate to help you and be with you forever— 17 the Spirit of truth. The world cannot accept him, because it neither sees him nor knows him. But you know him, for he lives with you and will be in you. 18 I will not leave you as orphans; I will come to you. 19 Before long, the world will not see me

anymore, but you will see me. Because I live, you also will live. 20 On that day you will realize that I am in my Father, and you are in me, and I am in you. 21 Whoever has my commands and keeps them is the one who loves me. The one who loves me will be loved by my Father, and I too will love them and show myself to them."

22 Then Judas (not Judas Iscariot) said, "But, Lord, why do you intend to show yourself to us and not to the world?"23 Jesus replied, "Anyone who loves me will obey my teaching. My Father will love them, and we will come to them and make our home with them. 24 Anyone who does not love me will not obey my teaching. These words you hear are not my own; they belong to the Father who sent me.

Take a moment to *absorb* those words. Let those words from the Son of God enter your soul as we prepare our hearts for the Word of God in the Book of James.

Now, before we move on, let's pray ...

Lord Jesus Christ, we love you, and we ask that you increase your Holy Spirit within us, as many of us are too weak to follow you as carefully as we should. Lord Jesus, give us your Holy Spirit in extra measure ... that we might show our love to you through our obedience to your teaching. Amen.

Friends, let's now return to the book of James. Here is the Word of the Lord from the Book of James, chapter 1, verses 19-27:

19 My dear brothers and sisters, take note of this: Everyone should be quick to listen, slow to speak and slow to become angry, 20 because human anger does not produce the righteousness that God desires. 21 Therefore, get rid of all moral filth and the evil that is so prevalent and humbly accept the word planted in you, which can save you.

22 Do not merely listen to the word, and so deceive yourselves. Do what it says. 23 Anyone who listens to the word but does not do what it says is like someone who looks at his face in a mirror 24 and, after looking at himself, goes away and immediately forgets what he looks like. 25 But whoever looks intently into the perfect law that gives freedom, and continues in it—not forgetting what they have heard, but doing it—they will be blessed in what they do.

26 Those who consider themselves religious and yet do not keep a tight rein on their tongues deceive themselves, and their religion is worthless. 27 Religion that God our Father accepts as pure and faultless is this: to look after orphans and widows in their distress, and to keep oneself from being polluted by the world.

James really hits the ground running here with a lesson that he is going to pound home repeatedly throughout his epistle, and that is this: *we must be ultra-careful with our words*. Our words represent us, and in many ways our words represent Jesus to those around us. If people find a huge disconnect between our words and our claim to Christianity, then they will become suspicious. As James will say later, in chapter 3 (vs. 11), "Can both fresh water and salt water flow from the same spring?"

In other words, how disciplined are you with your speech? Are you speaking too rashly, as James indicates in 1:19 when he says we should be "slow to speak"? Are you allowing anger to flow from your mouth?

James also asks us if "moral filth" is coming out of our mouths. I think we all understand what James is getting at.

- What harsh words did you use with a co-worker recently?

- What did you say behind that person's back?

- What "moral filth" came out of your mouth when you used those curse words?

- What does your tongue do when you lose your temper?

James has the harshest words of condemnation for those who have loose tongues. He says their religion is "worthless." In verse 26 he condemns those of us who have a loose tongue yet claim to be religious. Here's how James puts it: "Those who consider themselves religious and yet do not keep a tight rein on their tongues deceive themselves, and their religion is worthless."

This is the *third time* James has used the word "deceived" in the first chapter:

1. We deceive ourselves when we think we are the creators of our own good fortune. James 1:16-17 reminds us that "every" good gift is from God.

2. We deceive ourselves when we listen to God's word and neglect to *do* it. (James 1:22)

3. We deceive ourselves if we think we are religious yet fail to keep a tight rein on the tongue. (James 1:26)

In verse 21, James gives us a helpful analogy for listening to the word of God. He tells us to "humbly accept" it, as it is being "planted" in us. The Word of God should take root in us. It is just like a plant. We are vessels for God's Word—something pointed out by Jesus in John 14:20: "On that day you will realize that I am in my Father, and you are in me, and I am in you."

But ... and this is crucial ... before hearing the Word of God, we must "get rid of all moral filth" in our lives (vs. 21). We must be "humble" in order for it to get planted within us.

We also must realize that the Word of God can "save" us (v. 21). Did you catch that? There are three things we must do in order to "hear the Word of the Lord" well:

1. We must get rid of the moral filth and the sin in our lives.

2. We must become humble so that it gets planted into our hearts.

3. We must listen carefully to God's Word, for *it can save us*.

Were you lost in your sins before Christ came into your life? Those who responded "yes" know exactly what I'm talking about. You "once were lost, but now am found ... you were blind, but now you see."

Hearing the Word of God well requires *discipline*. We must purify ourselves so that we are not "double-minded" or "split-souled." We must be humble. The word of God has trouble getting into the arrogant heart.

And, finally, we need to realize the importance of preparing for the Word of the Lord ... It has the power to save your soul. It can save your life. It can save your family. It can save you. It can *literally save you*, as James makes clear.

In James 1:25, he pounds home the idea that listening and doing God's Word is a great blessing. God's laws might seem strict, but they actually bless our lives immensely. God's laws are "perfect," and do the right thing when we follow them in humble obedience. James says in verse 25 that if we actually put the Word of God into practice, then "we will be blessed in whatever we do." He also tells us in 1:25 that by doing God's will, we will have "freedom."

James was simply repeating something that the Lord Jesus taught frequently: his teaching provides freedom:

- If the Son sets you free, you will be free indeed. (John 8:36)

- Then you will know the truth, and the truth will set you free. (John 8:32)

- "The Spirit of the Lord is on me, because he has anointed me to proclaim good news to the poor. He has sent me to proclaim freedom for the prisoners and recovery of sight for the blind, to set the oppressed free. (Luke 4:18)

All of the biblical writers picked up on this teaching from Jesus. For instance, the apostle Paul said, "Now the Lord is the Spirit, and where the Spirit of the Lord is, there is freedom" (2 Cor. 3:17).

The apostle Peter said this in 1 Peter 2:16, "Live as free people, but do not use your freedom as a cover-up for evil; live as God's slaves."

In other words, listening carefully to God's Word is a blessing that brings freedom to your life. It may appear to confine you, or to limit you, or to inhibit you. But that is a lie of the devil. The Word of God is truth, and the truth will set you free.

Don't for a minute think that you will be constrained by following the Lord's will in your life. The truth is just the opposite. You will be so much better off by getting your life in synch with Christ's example.

Finally, James provides us with three very tangible and explicit examples of what "pure and faultless" religion looks like in the life of the believer (James 1:27):

1. Look after orphans in their distress;

2. Look after widows in their distress; and

3. Don't let yourself get "polluted by the world."

We could respond to James by saying, "clear enough." He would then come back and say, *"Then do what it says."*

Do you know any orphans? Do you know a kid who lost a parent? Do you know a kid whose parents aren't really "there"?

Do you know any widows? What might they need from you? What might be helpful to them? Do they need some work done in their home? Do they need some fellowship? Do they need your presence in their life?

And, thirdly, how do you get "polluted by the world?" Perhaps you got polluted without thinking too much about it. Dirty jokes at work. Filthy entertainment. Buying into the warped and sinful values of a secular world.

Let us all answer the call from James to "*Do what it says.*" Where are the orphans? Where are the widows? We must help them. How are we polluting ourselves? We must change habits in our lives so that we don't continue to get polluted by the world's values—which are usually at odds with true Christian faith.

Take-Homes from James 1:19-27

1. Show your love to Christ by obeying His Word.

2. Talk less, listen more.

3. Don't let the world continue to pollute you. Put a stop to it.

5. The Streets of Philadelphia

James 2:1-13

Superbowl Sunday is such a great time in America for those of us who love the game of football. Even people who don't like football somehow find themselves at Superbowl parties, just for the fun of it.

Sometimes it seems like the United States of America has fewer and fewer moments that bring us together. But, thankfully, we have the Superbowl—by far the most watched event in America each year. In recent years, over 100 million Americans have watched it. That's roughly 1 out of every 3 people in the nation who watched the game.

In 2023, the Superbowl was a spectacular game. It featured the Kansas City Chiefs and the Philadelphia Eagles—by far the two best teams in football that year. It had been a while since the #1 seed in the NFC faced the #1 seed in the AFC. It was a titanic clash of two very stout teams. The Chiefs barely pulled out the win, 38-35. But the Eagles fought hard, and were a most worthy opponent.

Oddly enough, I had just been in Philadelphia, just a few weeks before the game. I had never been there before. I attended a conference there with my beautiful 8-year-old daughter, Holly Joy. We had a blast.

We saw the place where the *U.S. Constitution* and the *Declaration of Independence* were created and signed. We saw the Liberty Bell with the famous crack in it. We saw the remains of the first President's House, home to George Washington and John Adams. We visited the home of Betsy Ross—who made the first official U.S. flag. We toured the U.S. Mint—where they make our coins.

We toured probably a dozen different churches, and came to love a city that is so crucial in American history. It is called "the city of brotherly love" because the Greek word *Philadelphia* means "brotherly love." The city represents a powerful unity that the early United States shared at that moment in our nation's history.

The night we arrived, my daughter and I were wide awake since we were on California time. We were staying at a hotel on Rittenhouse Square; it was the conference hotel where all of the lectures took place. After we got all checked in, we went walking towards City Hall, which, we later found out, is the world's largest freestanding masonry building. When it was completed, it was the world's tallest building. It is absolutely stunning.

As we walked, we saw many people scattered on the sidewalk, some passed out, some half alert, some in desperate need of help. There was one man whom I actually thought was dead. We stood there and watched for a long while, and eventually, he moved, just slightly. Numerous people asked us for money. One woman—probably my age—was laying in her own urine. One man was sprawled out on a manhole cover, as heat came up out of the subway system below.

At one point, my daughter and I came upon a teenage boy staring blankly at a statue. We asked him about the statue, and it became clear to us that he was absolutely *baked* out of his mind. We talked to two security officers standing nearby—both of them about 19 or 20 years old—and they said just to leave him alone. They said in downtown Philly you have to be careful because sometimes the drug addicts are unpredictable. They'll attack you. They told me to stay away from the boy—especially since I had a small child with me.

Our taxi driver told us he had a couple of friends who were shot and killed while driving. Being robbed in Philly while driving a taxi or Uber is common, he told us. He said Philly's downtown is "straight up dangerous." He warned us to be careful.

During and after that trip, I was reminded of Bruce Springsteen's famous, haunting song from 1994, called *Streets of Philadelphia*. That truly powerful song won the Academy Award that year for Best Original Song. It also cleaned up at the Grammys, winning Song of the Year, Best Rock Song, Best Rock Vocal Performance, and Best Song for Film or TV. I was in college in Texas in 1994, and knew very little about the city of Philadelphia. But I figured something had gone wrong in that once-great city. Already in 1994—when Springsteen released the song—it was clear that Philly's streets were in great peril.

The lyrics are powerful but in many ways brutal:

> I was bruised and battered
> I couldn't tell what I felt
> I was unrecognizable to myself
> Saw my reflection in a window
> And didn't know my own face
> Oh brother are you gonna leave me wastin' away
> On the streets of Philadelphia?

I walked the avenue, 'til my legs felt like stone
I heard the voices of friends vanished and gone
At night I could hear the blood in my veins
Just as black and whispering as the rain
On the streets of Philadelphia

Ain't no angel gonna greet me
It's just you and me my friend
And my clothes don't fit me no more
A thousand miles just to slip this skin

The night has fallen, I'm lyin' awake
I can feel myself fading away
So receive me brother with your faithless kiss
Or will we leave each other alone like this
On the streets of Philadelphia?

If you've walked the streets of Philadelphia, like Holly Joy and I did during those cold nights in January, you know exactly what I mean. The poverty is painful to see.

We stayed at a hotel on Rittenhouse Square. We were only a block from the depressed downtown area. But if you're walking around in the city, you suddenly find yourself in a completely different setting. Rittenhouse Square is considered to be one of the richest urban communities in the United States. Rittenhouse Park is beautiful and lush. A colleague took us to a coffee shop there. It was full of hipsters and yuppies, academicians and artists. It was an extremely happening place ... one of the most impressive coffee shops I have ever been to. It was classy, and looked historically significant both inside and out.

But just one block over: desperation. Crushing poverty. Hopeless addiction. And then suddenly you have Rittenhouse Square—true urban wealth—just steps away.

All of the experiences in Philly reminded me of what James had to say in chapter two, verses 1-13.

> My brothers and sisters ... believers in our glorious Lord Jesus Christ must not show favoritism. 2 Suppose a man comes into your meeting wearing a gold ring and fine clothes, and a poor man in filthy old clothes also comes in. 3 If you show special attention to the man wearing fine clothes and say, "Here's a good seat for you," but say to the poor man, "You stand there" or "Sit on the floor by my feet," 4 have you not discriminated among yourselves and become judges with evil thoughts?
>
> 5 Listen, my dear brothers and sisters: Has not God chosen those who are poor in the eyes of the world to be rich in faith and to inherit the kingdom he promised those who love him? 6 But you have dishonored the poor. Is it not the rich who are exploiting you? Are they not the ones who are dragging you into court? 7 Are they not the ones who are blaspheming the noble name of him to whom you belong?
>
> 8 If you really keep the royal law found in Scripture, "Love your neighbor as yourself," you are doing right. 9 But if you show favoritism, you sin and are convicted by the law as lawbreakers. 10 For whoever keeps the whole law and yet stumbles at just one point is guilty of breaking all of it. 11 For he who

said, "You shall not commit adultery," also said, "You shall not murder." If you do not commit adultery but do commit murder, you have become a lawbreaker.

12 Speak and act as those who are going to be judged by the law that gives freedom, 13 because judgment without mercy will be shown to anyone who has not been merciful. Mercy triumphs over judgment.

Catch that last sentence? *Mercy triumphs over judgment*.

Wow, that last little bit makes me want to pray: "Lord, have mercy upon us. We are a people with unclean hands and unclean lips. We discriminate. We judge. We favor. We look the other way. We neglect. We walk on by. We don't know what to do, O Lord. We realize, O Lord, that your mercy will be withheld from us if we don't show mercy to others. Have mercy on us, O Lord. And teach us *how to have* mercy. Forgive us, O Lord."

Friends, Christians are called to be a spiritual hospital, wherever God has planted us. In my case, I am adjacent to Los Angeles—with all of its glitz and glamor—but also its crushing poverty, rampant homelessness, violence, drugs, gangs, and mental illness.

As Christians, if we are going to be the hands and feet of Jesus, we must not discriminate. Rather, we must have *mercy*. Because the mercy that God extends to us is contingent upon the mercy we extend to the poor.

James reminds us that if we keep the whole law, yet stumble on this one, then we are guilty of breaking it all (2:10).

James chastises us for favoring some, and dehumanizing others. He calls for mercy, pure and simple.

One thing James does *not* say ... he does *not* say to dishonor the rich. Rather, James wants us to behave like God, and God is no respecter of persons. "God does not show favoritism" (Acts 10:34).

It is important to realize that the work of God requires resources. Those of us who have resources are compelled to reach out, to help, to serve, and, most importantly, to *have mercy*. We must use our blessings to reach out to the lost, to preach to the poor, to offer freedom to the prisoner, to give sight to the blind, to set the oppressed and addicted free, to follow Jesus closely in his mandate—made during what may have been his first sermon—when he said this:

"The Spirit of the Lord is on me because he has anointed me to proclaim good news to the poor. He has sent me to proclaim freedom for the prisoners and recovery of sight for the blind, to set the oppressed free, to proclaim the year of the Lord's favor" (Luke 4:18-19).

Friends, James lays it out very clearly: "If you really keep the royal law found in Scripture, 'Love your neighbor as yourself,' then you are doing right" (James 2:8).

To the rich Christians, we should say something like this: "lYou are so needed. Please join hands with us in the mission of Jesus Christ, the Great Physician. With the gifts you've received from God, you have the ability to make a *huge* difference. God has obviously blessed you. Now it's time for you to extend some mercy, and to support the work of God in this broken world."

To poor folks, we should say something like this: You are so welcome into the life of the church. You will never be treated less than anybody on account of your income. *You have our word* that we will try our best to give you the full dignity that you deserve as a child of God, made in his image.

Take-Homes from James 2:1-13

1. Treat everyone with dignity.

2. Love your neighbor as yourself.

3. "Judgment without mercy will be shown to anyone who has not been merciful" (2:13).

6. Well-Done is Better Than Well-Said

James 2:14-26

I love the game of football. I get excited every August as we start nearing the regular season for the NFL. One of my favorite things to do in the world is to recline in my chair and watch a Dallas Cowboys game, despite their lack of a Super Bowl in nearly 30 years!

As an alternative, I've had to learn how to enjoy watching other teams and other players. And the one player that we all had the privilege to watch for over two decades—from 2000 to 2022—was Tom Brady.

What does Tom Brady have to do with the book of James?

The answer to that question is found in James 2:26, which famously tells us that "faith without works is dead." And I would venture to say that Tom Brady is someone who understands the meaning of that expression.

Drafted in the year 2000, Brady was the 199th pick of that draft. He was taken by the New England Patriots late in the sixth round. He nearly went undrafted, as the seventh round is the final one. Imagine. Tom Brady—the greatest player in the history of football—nearly went undrafted.

But as we now know, Tom Brady's work ethic was Herculean. He outworked everybody else in the locker room. Year after year. He eventually went to 10 Super Bowls, and won 7 of them.

One of the most remarkable feats of Brady is that in 2020, he became the quarterback of the Tampa Bay Buccaneers, a team that had not even been to the playoffs in 12 years. Perpetual losers, there was little hope ... until Tom Brady arrived. The players began to believe in him and in themselves. Brady made it clear that just because he had already won 6 Super Bowl rings, he would not even think of letting up. Oh, and by the way, he was 43 years old at the time.

Here's what Brady Tweeted the day he signed with the Bucs:

> If there is one thing I have learned about football, it's that nobody cares what you did last year or the year before that ... you earn the trust and respect of those around through your commitment every single day. ... I have always believed that well-done is better than well-said, so I'm not gonna say much more. I'm just gonna get to work."

Brady had faith. But, more importantly, he got to work. And guess what happened to those hapless Buccaneers. They went from perpetual losers to winning the Super Bowl that very year, demolishing Patrick Mahomes and the Chiefs, 31 to 9. It wasn't a close game at all.

With Brady as their quarterback, the Bucs began to have some faith in themselves. However, Brady knew that faith was only the beginning. In order to get the job done, they needed *more* than faith. They needed to do some hard work.

Faith plus works was the winning formula. But *faith without works is dead*. Brady knew that. And that's why he's considered the greatest quarterback in the history of the game.

Here's what James says about these matters (James 2:14-26):

> 14 What good is it, my brothers and sisters, if someone claims to have faith but has no deeds? Can such faith save them? 15 Suppose a brother or a sister is without clothes and daily food. 16 If one of you says to them, "Go in peace; keep warm and well-fed," but does nothing about their physical needs, what good is it? 17 In the same way, faith by itself, if it is not accompanied by action, is dead.
>
> 18 But someone will say, "You have faith; I have deeds." Show me your faith without deeds, and I will show you my faith by my deeds. 19 You believe that there is one God. Good! Even the demons believe that—and shudder.
>
> 20 You foolish person, do you want evidence that faith without deeds is useless? 21 Was not our father Abraham considered righteous for what he did when he offered his son Isaac on the altar? 22 You see that his faith and his actions were working together, and his faith was made complete by what he did. 23 And the scripture was fulfilled that says, "Abraham believed God, and it was credited to him as righteousness," and he was called God's friend. 24 You see that a person is considered righteous by what they do and not by faith alone.

> 25 In the same way, was not even Rahab the prostitute considered righteous for what she did when she gave lodging to the spies and sent them off in a different direction? 26 As the body without the spirit is dead, so faith without deeds is dead.

Scholars and theologians have fiercely debated this passage for centuries. The central problem is whether James's emphasis on works is contrary to the apostle Paul's emphasis on salvation by faith, specifically in Ephesians 2:8-9: 8 For it is by grace you have been saved, through faith—and this is not from yourselves, it is the gift of God— 9 not by works, so that no one can boast.

However, when people quote this verse, they forget to continue the quote, into verse 10 (Ephesians 2:10): 10 For we are God's handiwork, created in Christ Jesus to do good works, which God prepared in advance for us to do.

In other words, when people say there is a conflict, upon closer inspection, we see that in the *very next verse*, Paul says the same thing that James says. The Christian needs both!

We need faith, *and* we need works. When we have faith, God meets us with His grace. But we *show* our faith through doing good works. And I have no doubt that Paul would say the exact same thing that James says—that *it is assumed* we will do good works if we actually have faith in Christ.

Faith without works is no faith at all. In fact, that kind of faith is dead. It's not a living faith.

Like Tom Brady said, "... well-done is better than well-said, so ... I'm just gonna get to work."

What James is trying to convey is that faith in Christ is only half of the story. If you're not doing something about it, then you don't have a living faith. Faith in Christ assumes you'll do good works for your faith.

James has a heart for the poor, the destitute, the widow, and the orphan. His compassion is probably best exemplified in James 1:27: Religion that God our Father accepts as pure and faultless is this: to look after orphans and widows in their distress and to keep oneself from being polluted by the world.

James also discusses, in 2:1-13, just how important it is that we *not* show favoritism to rich people. We must respect the poor as equals.

In James 2:14-17, he brings up the issue of the poor again, when he says this:

> What good is it, my brothers and sisters, if someone claims to have faith but has no deeds? Can such faith save them? 15 Suppose a brother or a sister is without clothes and daily food. 16 If one of you says to them, "Go in peace; keep warm and well-fed," but does nothing about their physical needs, what good is it? 17 In the same way, faith by itself, if it is not accompanied by action, is dead.

Once again, James takes us to the Streets of Philadelphia. He shows us in vivid imagery a poor person, without clothes, without food. And James chastises those people living in the rich sector of Philly, in Rittenhouse Square. "Go in peace; keep warm and well-fed." But they do nothing about the people on the next block over, a block full of hunger, poverty, violence, and desperation.

I have a very strong feeling that James is doing in chapter 2 what he does throughout his epistle: *he is referring to teachings that Jesus himself taught.*

If we turn back to the gospels, in Matthew 25:31-46, we encounter one of the most famous passages in the Bible about how we should deal with the poor, unclothed, and hungry. Let us remember ... these are the words of Jesus Christ. These are the words of God:

> 31 "When the Son of Man comes in his glory, and all the angels with him, he will sit on his glorious throne. 32 All the nations will be gathered before him, and he will separate the people one from another as a shepherd separates the sheep from the goats. 33 He will put the sheep on his right and the goats on his left.
>
> 34 "Then the King will say to those on his right, 'Come, you who are blessed by my Father; take your inheritance, the kingdom prepared for you since the creation of the world. 35 For I was hungry and you gave me something to eat, I was thirsty and you gave me something to drink, I was a stranger and you invited me in, 36 I needed clothes and you clothed me, I was sick and you looked after me, I was in prison and you came to visit me.'
>
> 37 "Then the righteous will answer him, 'Lord, when did we see you hungry and feed you, or thirsty and give you something to drink? 38 When did we see you a stranger and invite you in, or needing clothes and clothe you? 39 When did we see you sick or in prison and go to visit you?'
>
> 40 "The King will reply, 'Truly I tell you, whatever you did for one of the least of these brothers and sisters of mine, you did for me.'

41 "Then he will say to those on his left, 'Depart from me, you who are cursed, into the eternal fire prepared for the devil and his angels. 42 For I was hungry and you gave me nothing to eat, I was thirsty and you gave me nothing to drink, 43 I was a stranger and you did not invite me in, I needed clothes and you did not clothe me, I was sick and in prison and you did not look after me.'

44 "They also will answer, 'Lord, when did we see you hungry or thirsty or a stranger or needing clothes or sick or in prison, and did not help you?'

45 "He will reply, 'Truly I tell you, whatever you did not do for one of the least of these, you did not do for me.'

46 "Then they will go away to eternal punishment, but the righteous to eternal life."

Jesus *directly* connects feeding others, clothing others, accepting strangers, nurturing the sick back to health, and visiting prisoners ... Jesus connects all of this *directly with salvation*. That is powerful. That is big.

James does the same thing in his epistle. He says to his readers, "You have faith, great! But do you have the deeds to back it up?" James points out that even demons—fallen angels—have some orthodox *beliefs*. But what they don't have is the good deeds to confirm their faith in Christ. They only have belief. Thus, *their faith is dead*.

This mentality that we can just kick back and call ourselves Christians ... James calls it *"foolishness"* in verse 20. Our faith must be accompanied by good works for Jesus Christ. We must serve our neighbor. We must love him. We must help her. We must reach out to the poor. We must pitch in and do whatever we can to grow the church—the kingdom of God on the earth. We must give attention to prisoners. We must work hard to heal the people around us who have wounds—both physical and mental.

We must get to work. "Well-done is better than well-said."

James then reminds us of two Old Testament stories: Genesis 22 and Joshua chapters 2-6.

The first story deals with Abraham—who desperately wanted a son. Abraham was not perfect. He committed adultery with a woman because he lacked faith in God to provide him with a child. He also lied about Sarah being his sister, and badly endangered her. But, in the end, Abraham showed his faith through his works, when he was asked to sacrifice Isaac. But just as Abraham was about to sacrifice his son on the altar, an angel stopped him, and provided a ram for the sacrifice. Abraham's faith was tested, and he proved himself righteous by acting upon his faith.

Similarly, Rahab was not perfect. She was a young prostitute. She was a Gentile, and was living a sinful life. But she had heard of the God of the Israelites, and she put her faith in Him. She provided cover for the Israelite spies who had come to scope out the city of Jericho. She hid them and eventually helped them to escape. As a result, when the Israelites sieged and conquered the city of Jericho, they spared Rahab and her family.

And as a result, Rahab's family was assimilated and grafted into Jewish culture. Rahab quit her life of prostitution. She married a Jew named Salmon, and they had a son named Boaz—yes, that Boaz—the one who married Ruth. According to the genealogy of Jesus in Matthew chapter 1, Rahab's great, great-grandson was King David. In other words, Rahab is in the *royal line* of Abraham, Isaac, Jacob, David, Josiah, and eventually Joseph, who took Mary as his wife. And Mary's son Jesus was, and is, the long-awaited Jewish Messiah.

Just as our sins can carry on through generations, so also our good deeds can carry on through generations. The good that you do today will reverberate through many generations … to your children, and their children, and their children, and their children.

James speaks sternly when he says this (2:18), "Someone will say, 'You have faith; I have deeds.' Show me your faith without deeds, and I will show you my faith by my deeds."

Faith in Christ is so important. We are lost without it.

But what are we doing about it? I think we all can agree: "Well-done is better than well-said."

Take-Homes from James 2:14-26

1. Realize that faith in Christ is incomplete without good works.

2. Know that Jesus links salvation to good deeds … especially good deeds done for the poor.

3. Look forward to that day when Jesus says, "Well done, good and faithful servant. Come and share your master's happiness" (Matthew 25:21). Why is Jesus going to say this to us? It's because "well-done is better than well-said."

7. Taming the Tongue

James 3:1-18

Let us state the obvious: James—the brother of Jesus—can be extremely straightforward. But let us remember that Jesus could be like that, too. They had very similar teaching styles, and similar personality traits. They were both very direct communicators.

The image that is often portrayed of Jesus is that he was gentle and soft and kind. But it would be a mistake to think of Jesus strictly in those terms. Yes, Jesus had that gentle side to him, but he could also say things like this:

> 19 Therefore anyone who sets aside "one" of the least of these commands and teaches others accordingly will be called least in the kingdom of heaven, but whoever practices and teaches these commands will be called great in the kingdom of heaven. 20 For I tell you that unless your righteousness surpasses that of the Pharisees and the teachers of the law, you will certainly not enter the kingdom of heaven. (Matthew 5:19-21)

In that passage, Jesus sounds an awful lot like James. He urges teachers that they must practice what they preach. Jesus also emphasizes the importance of "doing what it says," just like James does. *Well-done* is far better than *well-said* in the minds of Jesus *and* James.

Indeed, some of the *most challenging* teachings in the Bible come from Jesus. Listen to this passage. It is a scene where Jesus is recruiting some disciples, and they actually asked for a little grace, so they could get some things done before they followed him. Here's the scene, from Luke 6:57-62:

> 57 As they were walking along the road, a man said to him, "I will follow you wherever you go."
>
> 58 Jesus replied, "Foxes have dens and birds have nests, but the Son of Man has no place to lay his head."
>
> 59 He said to another man, "Follow me."
>
> But he replied, "Lord, first let me go and bury my father."
>
> 60 Jesus said to him, "Let the dead bury their own dead, but you go and proclaim the kingdom of God."
>
> 61 Still another said, "I will follow you, Lord, but first let me go back and say goodbye to my family."
>
> 62 Jesus replied, "No one who puts a hand to the plow and looks back is fit for service in the kingdom of God."

Maybe you're thinking, "Man, that's harsh!" But let's remember, Jesus's ministry probably lasted only 3 years or so. One thing he *didn't* have was extra time. He was deeply committed to His mission, and if you had other things to do, then you were not fit to be part of his inner circle.

So why are we talking about how direct and even how harsh Jesus could sound at times?

It is because our friend James has some stern words for us in this chapter. It has to do with *taming our tongues*. Many of the writers of the Bible are deeply invested in this topic. From Genesis to Revelation, very few topics receive as much attention as this one.

The Bible urges us to get a firm handle on how we deal with our speech. And James offers up what is perhaps the clearest, best-known expression in scripture about how Christians should handle this problem. Here is the famous passage from James: James 3:1-18,

Not many of you should become teachers, my fellow believers because you know that we who teach will be judged more strictly. 2 We all stumble in many ways. Anyone who is never at fault in what they say is perfect, able to keep their whole body in check.

> 3 When we put bits into the mouths of horses to make them obey us, we can turn the whole animal. 4 Or take ships as an example. Although they are so large and are driven by strong winds, they are steered by a very small rudder wherever the pilot wants to go. 5 Likewise, the tongue is a small part of the body, but it makes great boasts. Consider what a great forest is set on fire by a small spark. 6 The tongue also is a fire, a world of evil

among the parts of the body. It corrupts the whole body, sets the whole course of one's life on fire, and is itself set on fire by hell.

7 All kinds of animals, birds, reptiles and sea creatures are being tamed and have been tamed by mankind, 8 but no human being can tame the tongue. It is a restless evil, full of deadly poison.

9 With the tongue we praise our Lord and Father, and with it we curse human beings, who have been made in God's likeness. 10 Out of the same mouth come praise and cursing. My brothers and sisters, this should not be. 11 Can both fresh water and salt water flow from the same spring? 12 My brothers and sisters, can a fig tree bear olives, or a grapevine bear figs? Neither can a salt spring produce fresh water.

13 Who is wise and understanding among you? Let them show it by their good life, by deeds done in the humility that comes from wisdom. 14 But if you harbor bitter envy and selfish ambition in your hearts, do not boast about it or deny the truth. 15 Such "wisdom" does not come down from heaven but is earthly, unspiritual, demonic. 16 For where you have envy and selfish ambition, there you find disorder and every evil practice.

17 But the wisdom that comes from heaven is first of all pure; then peace-loving, considerate, submissive, full of mercy and good fruit, impartial and sincere. 18 Peacemakers who sow in peace reap a harvest of righteousness.

Wow. There is a lot there. We could study this for the rest of our lives.

The bottom line is this: what we say to other people is extremely important. Sometimes I wonder if I'd be better off by taking the advice of Solomon, in Proverbs 17:27-28,

> 27 The one who has knowledge uses words with restraint,
> and whoever has understanding is even-tempered.
>
> 28 Even fools are thought wise if they keep silent,
> and discerning if they hold their tongues.

I don't know about you, but this passage from Proverbs, combined with James chapter three, makes me want to say quite a bit less than I currently do in life!

It is so true that if we talk too much, we almost inevitably end up saying things we probably shouldn't have said. Holding our tongue is a sign of maturity, of discernment and wisdom. Speaking too much often gets us into trouble. That's one of the reasons that James says teachers will be judged more strictly.

Let's unpack some of what James was getting at. He begins this passage by showing a little grace. He tells us that we are going to mess up. "We all stumble in many ways," he says in 3:2. Only a perfect person is able to keep it all in check. So right off the bat, James is letting us know that we are not perfect. While he wants us to be careful with our speech, we need to remember that we are human beings. We will struggle to get this right.

Next, James uses some analogies from farming, just like his brother Jesus routinely did. James talks about horses, and the bits in their mouths. Ever ridden a horse? You can control the horse with the reins, as the reins are attached by straps to a metal bit that is inserted into the horse's mouth. Normal riding horses weigh anywhere from 900 to 1800 pounds. And you can have serious control of that animal by using the bit, which is attached to the reins you hold. If you control the horse's mouth, then you can control all 1800 pounds of that beast.

Humans are no different. If you can control your tongue, then you can pretty much control your entire self.

The second analogy James uses is a ship's rudder. The rudder is a small blade that is underneath the boat, at the back end. It enables the helmsman to steer, control, and direct the vessel. Without a rudder, the ship can't operate properly, as there will be no ability to steer it. If your rudder breaks against rocks underneath, you might as well beach it because you'll have no control over the ship anymore.

Again, same with our tongue. It is a rudder. We steer ourselves with our tongue. It is *our* rudder.

The third analogy James offers is a forest fire, something I am all too familiar with in California, where I live.

- The Woolsey Fire in 2018 was started by a small electrical box that sparked.

- The 2018 Camp Fire that famously burned the town of Paradise was started by a faulty transmission line, causing $17 billion in damage, and 85 deaths. Over 50,000 people had to evacuate.

- In 2020, a cigarette butt started a major fire in Solano County—between San Francisco and Sacramento.

- The El Dorado fire in 2020 was started by a gender-reveal pyrotechnic mishap, killing a firefighter and causing over $40 million in damage.

- In 2022, there were 30 fires started in Contra Costa County alone (!) on the night of July 4. Investigators believe all of them were caused by small fireworks.

What is the point James is trying to make? He's trying to say that a lot of trouble can happen when someone let's loose with their mouth. Your tongue, that small muscle, can do irreparable damage. So be careful with it.

James tells us that our tongue can be a "world of evil." It can corrupt your entire body. It can set "the whole course of your life on fire." In other words, you can ruin your life with a loose, undisciplined tongue.

In verses 7-8, James tells us that all kinds of animals have been tamed throughout history. But "no human being can tame the tongue." He then calls it "a restless evil, full of deadly poison," obviously drawing the analogy to a snake.

Then in verses 9-12, James urges us to stop cursing. Stop praising God one day and then insulting people the next. He rephrases a famous teaching from Jesus in Matthew 12:33-37–which is perhaps the strongest warning in the entire Bible when it comes to our speech. Here's what our Lord said:

> 33 "Make a tree good and its fruit will be good, or make a tree bad and its fruit will be bad, for a tree is recognized by its fruit. 34 You brood of vipers, how can you who are evil say anything good? For the mouth speaks what the heart is full of. 35 A good man brings good things out of the good stored up in him, and an evil man brings evil things out of the

> evil stored up in him. 36 But I tell you that everyone will have to give account on the day of judgment for every empty word they have spoken. 37 For by your words you will be acquitted, and by your words you will be condemned."

In the final section of James's chapter on taming the tongue, he urges us to be people of wisdom, people who are peaceful. He warns us against "selfish ambition" (3:14). He warns us about being envious and boasting. All of this is "earthly, unspiritual, and demonic" (3:15).

James concludes this chapter by contrasting disorder with peace and wisdom. If we conduct our tongues with wisdom, then we will have peace. If we are considerate of others, and full of mercy, then we will see good fruit. If we aim for impartiality in our judgments, seasoned with sincerity, then we will enjoy peace, and we will "reap a harvest of righteousness" (3:18).

In other words, your life is probably going to go how your tongue goes. An undisciplined tongue will lead to disorder in your life, and possibly even destruction. But if you gain control of that little muscle inside your mouth—then you will experience good things. You will have more peace. And who in the world would choose disorder and chaos over peace?

I don't know about you, but I'm motivated to repent, and to become more aware of the words I use.

Finally, let us also remember that the tongue is capable of incredible amounts of good, too. The challenge from James is that we get control of that little muscle, and force it to submit to the way of peace, the way of righteousness ... the way of Jesus.

Take-Homes from James 3:1-18

1. Stop causing fires in your life with your tongue.

2. Put a bit in your mouth, and allow Jesus to control your speech.

3. Enjoy the peace that comes from a disciplined mouth.

8. Don't Become God's Enemy

James 4:1-12

Okay, a little test for some of you who have exceptional memories. Do you remember in a previous chapter when I discussed the word *dipsuchos*?

It is a word that is only used in the New Testament by our current author, James—the brother of Jesus. It is a great word, but it wasn't used much in that era. There are actually some Greek scholars who think James is the person who invented this word. And it is a splendid word. Now, for the test. What does *dipsuchos* mean? That word appears in our text from James that we are going to look at today, in James 4:8.

Okay, for those of you who answered *double-minded*, you got it right. Literally, the word means "of two souls," or "of two minds."

That word is at the heart of what we're going to talk about today. Are we committed to Christ and to his path? Or are we "*dipsuchos*–double-minded." Or, "split-souled."

I think I can speak for all of us when I say that we don't want to be double-minded, or possess a "double-soul." I want my soul to be completely dedicated to God. However, the history of *dipsuchos* goes way back.

It goes back to the Garden of Eden. Adam and Eve were given all the warning they needed. "Don't eat the fruit from this one tree." You can enjoy all the fruit from all of these other trees. They are all delicious. I command, you, however, you must not eat from this *one* tree. It is forbidden.

Then, stupidly, Adam and his wife start making their way over to that *one* tree that they're not supposed to eat from. And guess who is there to welcome them? Yes, Satan is there, transformed into a serpent. He persuades them to do it. They pluck the fruit, look at it, consider the cost, make a deal with the devil, and then *SMASH*—they bury their faces into it and eat it up. They loved it because it was so sweet and juicy. It was delicious! And it lasted like 10 seconds. Then they realized they had done something very, very wrong. Then the shame kicked in.

You've been there. You've heard the voice in the back of your head say, "Don't do it." You know it's wrong. Yet you keep walking in that direction ...

- Towards the party that has all kinds of shady stuff going on ...

- Towards the guy who is going to eat your heart and spit it out ...

- Towards the woman whom you know has a history of compromise ...

- Towards the money ... because there's a lot of it there ...

- Towards the friend that you know will pull you away from God.

You've done it. You saw the sin. You thought about it. You considered the consequences. Yet you made your way towards it. You stared at it. Then you reached out and grabbed it, and plucked it from the tree. You dove in with your teeth and enjoyed it with your mouth. It became yours for all but 10 seconds. Then, it was over. You're left empty-handed. Standing there. Wondering why you did it. You knew it. You saw the consequences from a mile away. Yet you dove in head first.

Dipsuchos. Doublemindedness. Why do we do it, as Christians? Why do we sin like that? Why do we almost *plan* to commit our sins sometimes? Do we have any respect for God and His teachings in the Bible whatsoever? Why do we choose to walk over there? Why do we choose that movie which will be full of curse words, killing, illicit relations, and nudity? Why do we walk over there and eat that stuff up?

This world is very, very sinful, folks. I don't have to list everything that is wrong with it. You know. We are a society that has become corrupted by our movies, by our entertainment, by our sinfully divided politics, and by our acceptance of broken relationships as if they're nothing.

We are a society that loves gossip. We prefer looking at our phones to actually talking with people sitting in the same room with us. We are a society that has chosen to serve money rather than God. We are a society that has conveniently forgotten the poor, the widows, the orphans, and the prisoners.

James has harsh words for his congregation there in Jerusalem around the year A.D. 45—only a decade or so after the death of Jesus. James tries to make it clear to his congregation. Let's see what he says ... not only to that congregation in Jerusalem, but let's open our ears—and our hearts—

and see what James has to say to each one of us. This text is from James 4:1-12.

> 1 What causes fights and quarrels among you? Don't they come from your desires that battle within you? 2 You desire but do not have, so you kill. You covet, but you cannot get what you want, so you quarrel and fight. You do not have because you do not ask God. 3 When you ask, you do not receive, because you ask with wrong motives, that you may spend what you get on your pleasures.
>
> 4 You adulterous people, don't you know that friendship with the world means enmity against God? Therefore, anyone who chooses to be a friend of the world becomes an enemy of God. 5 Or do you think Scripture says without reason that he jealously longs for the spirit he has caused to dwell in us? 6 But he gives us more grace. That is why Scripture says:
>
> "God opposes the proud
> but shows favor to the humble."
>
> 7 Submit yourselves, then, to God. Resist the devil, and he will flee from you. 8 Come near to God and he will come near to you. Wash your hands, you sinners, and purify your hearts, you double-minded. 9 Grieve, mourn and wail. Change your laughter to mourning and your joy to gloom. 10 Humble yourselves before the Lord, and he will lift you up.

11 Brothers and sisters, do not slander one another. Anyone who speaks against a brother or sister or judges them speaks against the law and judges it. When you judge the law, you are not keeping it, but sitting in judgment on it. 12 There is only one Lawgiver and Judge, the one who is able to save and destroy. But you—who are you to judge your neighbor?

Okay, this passage can be interpreted in a few different ways, but let me explain what I think is going on here. First, the passage is clearly bookended by James reprimanding people who are speaking against others in the church. The passage begins with James talking about the church quarreling and infighting. Surely that doesn't go on in the church? Your church has never struggled with this, right? No! Surely not! (I'm kidding!)

James basically opens this chapter by saying the church is quarreling about stuff because they all want to win the argument. People take sides. They get selfish. I want it THIS way. No, I want it THAT way.

- I want to sing the old hymns! Or ... I want to sing Phil Wickham, Bethel, and Elevation!

- I want carpet and pews. Or ... I want a hard floor with chairs that we can move around.

- I want a professional band up in front of the church. Or ... I want to keep the music chill and uncomplicated.

- I want our old preacher back. Or ... let's start another minister search.

- I want a little more hell fire and brimstone in the sermons! Or ... I want to hear good news, about God's grace and forgiveness.

You get the point. We disagree on stuff. And we always will.

But here's the problem. If those disagreements lead to people acting selfishly, then we really do have a problem. If people are leaving the church because of quarrels on the inside ... then we must go and seek them out, and apologize for anything we might have said that was hurtful to them. If someone left the church during the days of COVID-19, then the church needs to reach out to those people, and see why they left. Maybe they were hurt by someone's words, or by someone's actions. Maybe they couldn't handle the stress that COVID-19 brought into our churches.

Friends, we're going to have disagreements. And that's why we have to have a model for dealing with conflict in the church. And the Bible provides us with guidance. Personally, I like the consensus model. Consensus is a form of leadership where we listen to each other, and, in time, we make our moves as one body. There are very few *issues* that should split a church.

Okay, if someone says, "I don't believe Jesus is the son of God." Well, then we have a problem. That person has strayed from core Christian doctrine. But if we are talking about head-coverings, about who gives announcements, about how the music should go, about how much we should tithe, about who is qualified to be a pastor ... these are issues we can work out ... together. We talk about them. We walk shoulder to shoulder through these issues. And there will be many of them. But what James is addressing are the selfish quarrels. Some people will say, "I think the church should be like this, and I'm not compromising." Another will say, "I think Jim-Bob needs to be a deacon, and if he's not chosen, then I'm outta here." Someone else might say, "If the preacher mentions Tom Brady one more time in his sermons, then I'm done! Now ... *Go Cowboys*!

James ends this passage with some solutions. He reminds us that we've got to be kind and loving with each other. We can't judge one another. We can't speak against people, especially in the church. We are one, united body in Christ! There must be no division in the church.

We must walk together, shoulder to shoulder. If someone is thinking about leaving, then we need to do like Jesus says ... we need to leave the 99 sheep and go seek out the one who got away (Matthew 18:10-14). Literally, we should go to them and bring them back into the fold if at all possible. That's how we show our love. That's how the church grows.

When people feel valued, then they will feel like they belong to the body of Christ. And sometimes we must go to them and find them in order to get them back into the flock.

In verse 10, James gives us the secret sauce for all of this: humility. "Humble yourself before the Lord, and he will lift you up" (James 4:10). Don't get into the quarreling. Don't battle it out with other church members. Don't judge someone just because they view something a little differently than you do.

Let's be honest. What are the odds that we are all going to agree on everything? That's impossible! But we can find other solutions. Carpet or hard floor? Maybe both? Maybe some carpet here, and some hard floor over there.

I like this kind of music, and I will stomp out of here if you deviate from that. I only like sermons like this and I will quit the church if we start hearing sermons like that. I like announcements to go like this, and if someone doesn't do it the way I like it, then I'm outta here.

Folks, that's so wrong. It's selfish. What's Christianity all about? It's about a God who created people because he wanted to have fellowship with them. But we are sinners. So, God sent His son to bring us back into the fold ... that we might be in His family forever. He sought us out ... just like the shepherd leaves the 99 to get to the one who is lost.

Don't let the *minor stuff* become your *major stuff*. Don't major in the minors. Don't get all angry about externals. Don't get arrogant. Don't say things like, "I won't back down!" Be humble. Be willing to concede. Very few issues in the church are worth dying over. Here and there, yes. If heresy slips in, then wallop it! But most things are negotiable because they're not salvation issues.

Another important verse in James 4:1-12 is this: "Come near to God and he will come near to you. Wash your hands, you sinners, and purify your hearts, you double-minded." There we get our word again: *dipsuchos*.

The Bible teaches that the world is in some sense the realm of Satan. At least Satan is allowed, by God, to roam through it and wreak havoc in it. And according to the New Testament, if you are a friend to the world, then you are God's enemy (4:4).

In the church, we function with humility. We don't demand that we each get our own way. We don't judge one another when one of us sees something differently than we do. We don't leave when we have an argument over some superficial matter. We don't act with arrogance.

Rather, we humble ourselves. We promise to never speak ill of each other. Could you make that promise? Could you actually say, "I will never speak ill of anyone in my church ever again"?

James ends this section of scripture by saying (4:17), "If anyone, then, knows the good they ought to do and doesn't do it, it is sin for them." In context, James is saying this to us: "Now ... go and repair the rifts you caused. Go and stitch up that problem you have with someone. Apologize. Humble yourself. Repent of your sin. Do something good for a change. Don't keep quarreling about stuff."

Instead, James tells us, "Go and do some good for that person. That's how you fix a problem. *Go do something good for them!*"

Take-Homes from James 4:1-12

1. Try hard to get along with people. Stop quarreling.

2. Make a firm decision for God. Don't be a "split soul."

3. Instead of talking bad about somebody ... *go do something good* for them.

9. The Wealthy Elephant in the Room

James 4:13–5:6

This text is very challenging for some people. It is about the pride and arrogance that comes from wealth. Why did I choose such a strange title for the chapter? I chose it because *we are* the elephant in the room. We've been blessed in so many ways, materially speaking.

- We live in the United States of America, one of the wealthiest nations to ever exist on the earth. Possibly, *the* wealthiest.

- Many reading this chapter have good jobs with good salaries.

- Many of us have so much stuff that we could probably give a bunch of it away.

- Many of us live such comfortable lives that most of the world can only dream about.

Some of you are probably thinking, "Okay, are you going to blast me because I've saved up money? Are you going to do a Marxist critique of me? Are you going to try to make me feel bad simply because I worked hard, lived a frugal life, took care of my family, and was responsible enough to acquire a good nest egg for my retirement?"

Let me just say on the front end, "*No. I am not going to do that.*" And I'm *definitely* not a Marxist. Karl Marx caused more damage than nearly anybody in the last 200 years of history. The nations that followed his atheistic theories were devastated in the 20th century. It was not a pretty picture: the Soviet Union, Communist China, Castro Cuba, North Korea, and others.

So, no. I am not going to point fingers. But I *am* going to quote scripture. And I'm going to apply them to us, and to our situation today. We ignore scripture at our own peril. Let's open our Bibles and see what the Holy Spirit has to say through his servant James—the brother of Jesus. And let us also see what James and others have to say about the potentially negative effects of *avarice*, *mammon*, *hoarding*, *exploiting*, and the like.

The first text is from James 4:13–5:6:

> 13 Now listen, you who say, "Today or tomorrow we will go to this or that city, spend a year there, carry on business and make money." 14 Why, you do not even know what will happen tomorrow. What is your life? You are a mist that appears for a little while and then vanishes. 15 Instead, you ought to say, "If it is the Lord's will, we will live and do this or that." 16 As it is, you boast in your arrogant schemes. All such boasting is evil. 17 If anyone, then, knows the good they ought to do and doesn't do it, it is sin for them.

5 Now listen, you rich people, weep and wail because of the misery that is coming on you. 2 Your wealth has rotted, and moths have eaten your clothes. 3 Your gold and silver are corroded. Their corrosion will testify against you and eat your flesh like fire. You have hoarded wealth in the last days. 4 Look! The wages you failed to pay the workers who mowed your fields are crying out against you. The cries of the harvesters have reached the ears of the Lord Almighty. 5 You have lived on earth in luxury and self-indulgence. You have fattened yourselves in the day of slaughter. 6 You have condemned and murdered the innocent one, who was not opposing you.

Okay, before we get into the lessons that can be extracted from this pretty indicting scripture, let's look at similar passages in the Bible.

One thing that cannot be argued against: James knew the Old Testament very well. He also knew the teachings of Jesus very well. And in virtually every line of James' epistle, you are going to hear echoes of Old Testament passages, especially the book of Proverbs and the Prophets. You are also going to hear very clear references to the teachings of James's brother.

Let's examine a passage from Isaiah. It is similar to James in how it provides examples of how the rich are living, and it doesn't paint a rosy picture. The text is Isaiah 3:13–26. It is a scene of the Lord presiding over a courtroom full of people, and God makes His judgment against some of the people there:

13 The Lord takes his place in court;
he rises to judge the people.
14 The Lord enters into judgment
against the elders and leaders of his people:
"It is you who have ruined my vineyard;
the plunder from the poor is in your houses.
15 What do you mean by crushing my people
and grinding the faces of the poor?"
declares the Lord, the Lord Almighty.

16 The Lord says,
"The women of Zion are haughty,
walking along with outstretched necks,
flirting with their eyes,
strutting along with swaying hips,
with ornaments jingling on their ankles.
17 Therefore the Lord will bring sores on the heads of the women of Zion;
   the Lord will make their scalps bald."

18 In that day the Lord will snatch away their finery: the bangles and headbands and crescent necklaces, 19 the earrings and bracelets and veils, 20 the headdresses and anklets and sashes, the perfume bottles and charms, 21 the signet rings and nose rings, 22 the fine robes and the capes and cloaks, the purses 23 and mirrors, and the linen garments and tiaras and shawls.

24 Instead of fragrance there will be a stench;
   instead of a sash, a rope;
instead of well-dressed hair, baldness;
   instead of fine clothing, sackcloth;

instead of beauty, branding.
25 Your men will fall by the sword,
your warriors in battle.
26 The gates of Zion will lament and mourn;
destitute, she will sit on the ground.

The context of Isaiah is similar to the context of James. You have people who are wealthy, and you have people who are poor. And the wealthy ones seem not to care about the needs of those who live in extreme lack.

The next two passages we should consider are from Jesus himself. Let's remember that when we listen to Jesus, we are unmistakably listening to God. The first reading is Luke 12:13–21:

13 Someone in the crowd said to him, "Teacher,
tell my brother to divide the inheritance with me."

14 Jesus replied, "Man, who appointed me a judge
or an arbiter between you?" 15 Then he said to
them, "Watch out! Be on your guard against all
kinds of greed; life does not consist in an abundance of possessions."

16 And he told them this parable: "The ground of a
certain rich man yielded an abundant
harvest. 17 He thought to himself, 'What shall I do?
I have no place to store my crops.'

18 "Then he said, 'This is what I'll do. I will tear
down my barns and build bigger ones, and there I
will store my surplus grain. 19 And I'll say to my-

self, "You have plenty of grain laid up for many years. Take life easy; eat, drink and be merry."'

20 "But God said to him, 'You fool! This very night your life will be demanded from you. Then who will get what you have prepared for yourself?'

21 "This is how it will be with whoever stores up things for themselves but is not rich toward God."

Did you see the connections between James and Jesus in that text? *Hoarding* is the central problem in the story of the rich fool. He's hoarding without giving anything to people. He is saving and saving, but for what? He's not helping *anyone*. He's saving just to save. His investments are solely for the sake of his own pleasure, so he can "... take life easy, eat, drink, and be merry" (vs. 19).

The second key statement from Jesus on the concept of wealth comes from Matthew 6:19–21, 24, right there in the Sermon on the Mount:

19 "Do not store up for yourselves treasures on earth, where moths and vermin destroy, and where thieves break in and steal. 20 But store up for yourselves treasures in heaven, where moths and vermin do not destroy, and where thieves do not break in and steal. 21 For where your treasure is, there your heart will be also.

24 "No one can serve two masters. Either you will hate the one and love the other, or you will be devoted to the one and despise the other. You cannot serve both God and money.

Once again, the issue seems to be about hoarding wealth. Jesus is addressing the purposelessness of accumulating vast sums of money that help nobody.

Why? Because if you hoard like that, then you're not helping the people around you, as you should. If God has blessed you with wealth, then use it for good. Bless others with it. If you are saving just to save, then you are a slave to your money, rather than a servant to the living God, who both gives and takes away.

Friends, what is being addressed in these passages in the concept of *avarice*. This is an old English term that's not used much anymore. According to the dictionary, the word "avarice" means: "... extreme greed for wealth or material gain." Another definition is this: "... insatiable greed for riches; inordinate, miserly desire to gain and hoard wealth."

And while we're talking about avarice, let's not forget the words of the great apostle Paul, who says this in: 1 Timothy 6:17–19:

> 17 Command those who are rich in this present world not to be arrogant nor to put their hope in wealth, which is so uncertain, but to put their hope in God, who richly provides us with everything for our enjoyment. 18 Command them to do good, to be rich in good deeds, and to be generous and willing to share. 19 In this way they will lay up treasure for themselves as a firm foundation for the coming age, so that they may take hold of the life that is truly life.

I really like how Paul expresses it there. He doesn't condemn rich people simply for being rich. He encourages them, rather, to put their hope in God, to do *good* things with their money. To "*be generous and willing to share.*" If wealthy folks do good deeds with their money, then they will lay up treasures for themselves in heaven. And they'll also help the people on earth who are in need.

We've all heard stories about people who win the lottery and then their lives become so complicated afterward. They get a divorce, and lose half of their winnings. People constantly surround them, wanting a slice of the pie. They spend way more than they should. Often, their lives end up pretty miserable. They became super rich, but the quality of their lives may have actually declined.

I've often thought that if I played the lottery (which I don't) and won a ton of money, then I'd have a field day giving all of that money away to people—unsuspecting homeless folks, people I know who struggle, families with several children, people who lose their job and can't afford to lose their job, people in my world who are clearly struggling to pay their bills. It would be so fun to help people!

Or would it? Would I hoard? Would I keep all that money in Wells Fargo? Or in some offshore bank? Would I simply use my wealth to take vacations to exotic places, buy my dream cars, and simply hold on to that cash, so I could "eat, drink, and be merry," without a thought in the world about the poor in my life? Would I neglect the Lord's kingdom, knowing that if the preacher found out about my lottery winnings, then he'll surely expect some BIG contributions from me?

What would I do? What would you do?

James is doing what he often does: he is addressing our arrogance and selfishness. He's chastising those people who proudly talk about their voyages to far off places. He's coming down hard on people who "carry on business and make money" (4:13) without having any concern about the Lord.

They brag about everything they do, when in reality, they should have a spirit of humility that says, "If it's God's will, then maybe I'll do this or that" (4:13).

James must have had this passage in mind, from Proverbs 27:1,

Do not boast about tomorrow, for you do not know what a day may bring.

James then gives us this wonderful little sentence that often goes missed, in James 4:17, "If anyone, then, knows the good they ought to do and doesn't do it, it is sin for them."

At first glance, that sentence looks out of place in the context of James 4. But it actually fits perfectly. James is warning us that if we see something we need to do with our money, and we refuse to help, then we are sinning. Again, *if there is something you need to help out with, and you refuse to do anything about it, then you've sinned.* You've neglected someone who needed help. Think about the story of the Good Samaritan.

It is pretty clear that James also had Psalm 39:5 on his mind when he wrote his epistle.

> You have made my days a mere handbreadth;
> the span of my years is as nothing before you.
> Everyone is but a breath,
> even those who seem secure.

James is surely looking at that passage in the Psalm 39 when he says in 4:14, "What is your life? You are a mist that appears for a little while and then vanishes."

The apostle Peter picks up on this concept, too, when he writes the following in 1 Peter 1:24-25,

> "All people are like grass,
>   and all their glory is like the flowers of the field;
> the grass withers and the flowers fall,
>   but the word of the Lord endures forever."

Friends, we've looked at a lot of scripture in this chapter. We've considered the words of James, Isaiah, Jesus, Paul, David, and Peter. I think we all know the message that's being conveyed about wealth. *Many of us reading this are the wealthy elephants in the room.* Maybe we're not multi-millionaires, but you must admit, most of us have it pretty good in the United States. Just travel to the Global South, as I often do, and you'll see what we have. The disparity is huge.

The question for us is, "What will we do about economic disparity?" We can hoard. We can "eat, drink, and be merry." We can take refuge in our possessions and sizable savings. Or we can commit to being a light to the people around us by using our wealth as a blessing in our communities. In our churches. With the hurting.

James says in 4:17, "If anyone, then, knows the good they ought to do and doesn't do it, it is sin for them." If you happen to be someone who has wealth, then I encourage you to resist the urge to hoard, and find some ways to bless people. That's it. No judgment. No guilt. Just find a way to bless the people around you. You've worked hard and God has blessed you. Now it's time for you to bless others.

Take-Homes from James 4:13-5:6

1. Don't hoard.

2. If you're wealthy, you're not a bad person. You just have responsibilities.

3. Acknowledge God with every penny you receive, and with every breath you take. Even your next breath is God's allowance to you.

10. Patience Means Firmness of Faith

James 5:7-12

In this chapter, we look at a powerful text from James that will be encouraging to you, and I mean that word very literally: *encouraging*. This lesson is intended to strengthen your heart. It is my hope that this lesson gives you courage to *stand firm* against the forces of evil that come your way. I hope this lesson will embolden you to live the Christian life better, to conform your life more to what Jesus asks of you, and to *do what it says*.

Let's now dive into James 5:7-12.

> 7 Be patient, then, brothers and sisters, until the Lord's coming. See how the farmer waits for the land to yield its valuable crop, patiently waiting for the autumn and spring rains. 8 You too, be patient and stand firm, because the Lord's coming is near. 9 Don't grumble against one another, brothers and sisters, or you will be judged. The Judge is standing at the door!

10 Brothers and sisters, as an example of patience in the face of suffering, take the prophets who spoke in the name of the Lord. 11 As you know, we count as blessed those who have persevered. You have heard of Job's perseverance and have seen what the Lord finally brought about. The Lord is full of compassion and mercy.

12 Above all, my brothers and sisters, do not swear—not by heaven or by earth or by anything else. All you need to say is a simple "Yes" or "No." Otherwise you will be condemned.

I want to draw your attention to a most important expression in this text. It occurs in verse 8. The NIV translates it, "stand firm." That is an expression the NIV translators chose to use. Although it is indeed a good translation of the *expression*, it is not a *literal* translation from the Greek. The Greek words are "sterizo kardias." You know the word "kardia." Think of "cardiology." Or a "cardiac arrest." The other word is a form of the verb "sterizo" which means "strengthen." So, the literal translation is "strengthen your hearts."

I want to encourage you with that expression—*strengthen your hearts*—or, *stand firm*, because, in a way, it summarizes today's text. Sometimes we have to put our big boy and big girl pants on and get strong.

We have to strengthen our insides. We have to be firm. We can't waver. We have to be resolute. This all requires courage and inner strength. There is a time to be supple and malleable, and there is a time to *stand firm*. And James is calling us to the latter.

We are to *strengthen our hearts* and firm up our insides when we are persecuted; when we feel like laying in bed all day sucking our thumbs; when we feel like shrinking back and taking cover; when we feel like folding.

James says, "No." *You stand up.* Be patient. You have the strength of the Lord. You have God on your side. Greater is He that is in me! I can do all things through Christ, who gives me strength. God causes all things to work out for the good for those who love Him.

I want to bring up a song here. One of my favorite pop songs is Tom Petty's hit "I won't back down." Listen to these lyrics. They are so appropriate here.

> Well, I won't back down; No I won't back down
> You could stand me up at the gates of Hell
> But I won't back down
>
> No, I'll stand my ground; Won't be turned around
> And I'll keep this world from draggin' me down
> Gonna stand my ground; And I won't back down
>
> Hey baby; There ain't no easy way out
> Hey I, will stand my ground;
>
> And I won't back down
>
> Well, I know what's right; I got just one life
> In a world that keeps on pushin' me around;
>
> But I'll stand my ground; And I won't back down
>
> Hey baby; There ain't no easy way out
> Hey I, will stand my ground; And I won't back down

Now, I don't know about the religious beliefs of Tom Petty. But one thing I do know is that those words are powerful. They are a testament to standing strong when you know what's right. When there is resistance to your commitments to God, you have to stand up for yourself. This culture is going to push you around. And there's no easy way to go about this. Sometimes you have to stand your ground. Don't back down. Especially when you are being pushed around by the *evil one*.

The apostle Paul gives an absolutely beautiful testament to this godly firmness in Ephesians 6:10-18, when he writes the following:

> 10 Finally, be strong in the Lord and in his mighty power. 11 Put on the full armor of God, so that you can take your stand against the devil's schemes. 12 For our struggle is not against flesh and blood, but against the rulers, against the authorities, against the powers of this dark world and against the spiritual forces of evil in the heavenly realms. 13 Therefore put on the full armor of God, so that when the day of evil comes, you may be able to stand your ground, and after you have done everything, to stand. 14 Stand firm then, with the belt of truth buckled around your waist, with the breastplate of righteousness in place, 15 and with your feet fitted with the readiness that comes from the gospel of peace. 16 In addition to all this, take up the shield of faith, with which you can extinguish all the flaming arrows of the evil one. 17 Take the helmet of salvation and the sword of the Spirit, which is the word of God.

18 And pray in the Spirit on all occasions with all kinds of prayers and requests. With this in mind, be alert and always keep on praying for all the Lord's people.

In other words. Stand your ground. Don't back down.

We could also say, as James says, "Strengthen your heart." Now is *not* the time for weakness. Now is the time to harden your insides.

There is another key idea that James is trying to express in this text ... and that is *patience*.

Farmers have to wait months at a time ... looking out the window. Waiting for the rains. Thinking. Having to be prepared if the rains don't come. Trying to be strong.

Job. He was *famous* for his patience. He was tested by the devil. Literally tortured by Satan. You know the story, Job was a righteous man. It says in Job that "he feared God and shunned evil" (Job 1:1). However, one day, the angels appeared before God. Satan was there, too. And God asked Satan, "Have you considered my servant Job? There is no one on earth like him; he is blameless and upright, a man who fears God and shuns evil." And that's when Satan made his move to start torturing this man of God.

But Job wasn't the only one tortured by Satan in scripture. Listen to what the apostle Paul said in 2 Corinthians 12:7b-10:

Therefore, in order to keep me from becoming conceited, I was given a thorn in my flesh, a messenger of Satan, to torment me. 8 Three times I pleaded with the Lord to take it away from me. 9 But he said to me, "My grace is sufficient for you, for my power is made perfect in weakness." Therefore, I will boast all the more gladly about my weaknesses, so that Christ's power may rest on me. 10 That is why, for Christ's sake, I delight in weaknesses, in insults, in hardships, in persecutions, in difficulties. For when I am weak, then I am strong.

Friends, we are each going to have our turn. Each one of us will be attacked by Satan. If you live long enough, then there will be some kind of adversity that will come your way.

- The lawsuit that comes out of nowhere.

- The untimely death of someone you truly cared about.

- The struggle with serious illness.

- The stressful situation that arises in your workplace.

- The person you thought was a friend was not quite a friend.

These situations happen. Satan comes after you. Our battle is not against flesh and blood. The battle is spiritual.

Now let's talk a minute about *patience*. Sometimes we have to strengthen our hearts and be patient. Sometimes we have to just dig in, like a soldier in the trenches. We just have to dig in and wait for the Lord. Like a farmer waiting for rain. Like Job, trying to get through the death of loved ones, the loss of his wealth, and eventually the sudden collapse of his own health. Sometimes the only way we can honor God is through our patience, and our perseverance.

We must have patience that God will make things right. After all, He is our father. And, as James says, he is "full of compassion and mercy."

Sometimes we must stand in there and persevere. As James says in 5:10, we are called to be "an example of patience in the face of suffering."

Then James mentions some prophets who were persecuted. There were so many of them throughout scripture.

- Joseph was rejected by his brothers and sold as a slave.

- Hosea's wife was unfaithful to him, and he suffered through her acts of promiscuity.

- Stephen was stoned to death in the earliest years of Christianity.

- Paul went through all kinds of punishment before he was beheaded.

- Peter was crucified upside down.

- Jesus, the Lord, was tortured beyond all measure before His death.

Indeed, both the prophets and the Son of God suffered. But, as James points out, "You have seen what the Lord finally brought about" (5:11):

- Joseph became one of the great leaders of the Egyptian Empire.

- Job was blessed greatly after his period of trial and persecution.

- Stephen was welcomed into heaven.

- Jesus was resurrected to glory and now sits at the right hand of the Father.

God caused all things to work together for the good because they truly loved Him. God rewarded them for their perseverance.

As with the prophets, we, too, will go through terrible storms in this life. Huge challenges will come your way. And there are several different ways you can meet those challenges.

But the way James asks us to meet them is through *patience and perseverance*. We must *strengthen our hearts*. We must *stand firm*.

People are watching us. People want to see how Christians respond to testing, to temptations, to torture from the evil one. People want to see how Christians handle adversity. How we deal with our disappointments and our anger. People are watching us, waiting to see how disciples of Jesus handle these kinds of challenges.

All human beings suffer. But Christians handle it differently. We have a divine source of comfort: the Holy Spirit of God. We have a living relationship with Jesus Christ. And this makes all the difference.

If we turn to our faith during our trials, then we will set an example for non-Christians. We are modeling our faith for the people around us.

The famous pastor Rick Warren lost his son to mental illness-induced suicide. Rick and his wife Kay were devastated. But they persevered. And they still hurt, but they have chosen to use that pain for God's glory. Here's what Pastor Warren wrote about dealing with pain:

Your deepest life message will come out of your deepest pain. The world doesn't need to see Christians who are perfect or have it all together. They need something real and authentic. They need to see Christians who are patient in pain, who walk faithfully in suffering.

Every area of your life where you've experienced pain is a testimony. Has God helped you work your way out of deep debt? That was painful—but it's also a testimony. Has God helped you patiently endure chronic pain? That's a testimony. Anywhere you've had pain and experienced God's help is a testimony.

I beg you not to waste your pain; don't waste your hurt. People all around you are going through the very thing you've already gone through, and they need your help. They need you to comfort them.

The greatest witness of God's love in all history was not Jesus' perfect life, his sermons, his miracles, or his stories. It was his suffering.

God can use your faithfulness in suffering to great effect in someone's life. In fact, your faithfulness in suffering could be your greatest witness![1]

Let's close this chapter by looking at the powerful and hopeful words of James 5:7, "Be patient, then, brothers and sisters, until the Lord's coming."

Take-Homes from James 5:7–12.

1. Find that inner strength within you.

2. Pray for patience.

3. Persevere. God will work it out for good. Trust him.

---

[1] Rick Warren, "Turn Your Pain into a Testimony," *PastorRick.com*, March 22, 2023, https://pastorrick.com/turn-your-pain-into-a-testimony/.

11. Prayer, Confession, and Healing

James 5:13-20

The last section of the Epistle of James focuses upon prayer. Prayer should be like breathing in the life of the Christian. We should pray as we live our lives, as we wake up in the morning, as we eat our food, as we get ready for the day, as we go about our work, as we wind down in the evening, and as we place our head on the pillow.

We are Christians. We should be praying constantly. As the apostle Paul says in 1 Thessalonians 5:17-18, "Pray continually, giving thanks in all circumstances."

We should constantly be giving thanks to God. It will tenderize our hearts. Instead of hardness of heart, we will have softer hearts. We will have grateful hearts. We will be thankful for what God has done in our lives, rather than being irritated and feeling victimized about what God hasn't done in our lives.

We pray, and we give thanks. As Christians, we don't just give thanks at mealtime (but let us not forget to do it then), but we give thanks to God *often*, for all sorts of reasons, and for all kinds of blessings that most people don't recognize as coming from God.

In the New Testament, many of the epistles end with words about prayer. And the Book of James is no exception. James provides some wonderful words on prayer, but he does something very interesting: *James links prayer to healing and confession.* Let's have a look at James 5:13-20:

> 13 Is anyone among you in trouble? Let them pray. Is anyone happy? Let them sing songs of praise. 14 Is anyone among you sick? Let them call the elders of the church to pray over them and anoint them with oil in the name of the Lord. 15 And the prayer offered in faith will make the sick person well; the Lord will raise them up. If they have sinned, they will be forgiven. 16 Therefore confess your sins to each other and pray for each other so that you may be healed. The prayer of a righteous person is powerful and effective.
>
> 17 Elijah was a human being, even as we are. He prayed earnestly that it would not rain, and it did not rain on the land for three and a half years. 18 Again he prayed, and the heavens gave rain, and the earth produced its crops.
>
> 19 My brothers and sisters, if one of you should wander from the truth and someone should bring that person back, 20 remember this: Whoever turns a sinner from the error of their way will save them from death and cover over a multitude of sins.

It is clear that in this passage, James is telling us to pray. But that's not all. He's telling us *why* we should pray. And he's also helping us to develop a *context for why* we pray.

It's not enough just to say, "Pray." James provides an understanding of the greater context *surrounding* prayer. Of course, many Christians have had the opportunity to do an entire study of prayer, looking at what Jesus and the New Testament writers have to say about prayer. But right now, let's focus in on what James is saying.

James asks if any of us are in trouble. Are you? Are you troubled by anything? Is there something in your life that is particularly intimidating? Is there a person with whom you are having troubled relations? Perhaps a vexing situation that you don't quite know how to solve? Perhaps your spirit is troubled with mental or spiritual struggles, and you don't know where to turn?

James makes it clear. You need to pray. Often times, we go to every *other* source, and eventually, we say something like, "Well, at least I can pray." That is not the right attitude. Prayer is not a "least" activity. Pray is a "most" activity. It is knocking on the door of the great King, and He lets you in, and you sit down before Him, and you humbly ask Him for something. Prayer is nothing less than talking—one on one—with the Creator of the universe.

Recently, I had an exceptional opportunity. I sat down with the President of Pepperdine University, where I am employed. I wasn't alone. There were seven of us faculty, and we took him out to eat at a local restaurant there in Malibu. We had a wonderful time eating, discussing, and sharing our thoughts on many different issues. It was an honor. The president of a major university, sitting down with us for three hours, and just being real. We spoke openly. It was a wonderful moment because we took off our masks, and just visited with the man in charge of our institution. It was a great opportunity.

But talking with the *Creator* is on another level. Our God is in control of the heavens. All that exists is subject to His authority. The earth and the stars and the planets exist because of His act of creation. Great men suddenly drop dead because He is the God who gives, and He is the God who takes away.

And we get to bow down before Him. We get to spend *as much time with Him as we want*! Can you imagine? It is *absolutely extraordinary* that we have been given this opportunity to go to the Creator in confidence.

In 5:13, James then tells us to sing songs of praise. When we have the opportunity to praise, let's praise God with all our strength, and deep down in our souls. Corporate worship with fellow believers is such a blessing. It is an opportunity to praise God alongside people who share our love for Him.

Then in James 5:14-15, James gives some very interesting advice. He says that if someone is sick, then they should "... call the elders of the church to pray over them and anoint them with oil in the name of the Lord. And the prayer offered in faith will make the sick person well; the Lord will raise them up."

What do we make of this? Is this literal?

Recently, I did an interview for a newspaper. They asked me if I believe God works in the world. I said, "But of course. Why else do we pray?" So, yes, of course we pray because we believe God works in the world! If the Bible is clear on anything, it is this: We need to pray to God on all occasions, especially when troubled or sick.

Will God actually heal the person we pray for? Let me ask you ... Has God ever come to your aid? Has He ever healed your sickness, whether mental or physical? Has God answered your prayers for healing before? Of course He has! The Bible calls Jesus our *doctor*, our *physician*, in Mark 2:17. So, naturally, we turn to the Lord when we need healing–whether physical, mental, or spiritual. We turn to Christ when we need healing because Christ has proven that He can heal people.

James adds some more ideas for us. He suggests the elders gather around a sick person, and pray over them. The elders should anoint the person with oil. Olive oil had many uses in Bible times; two of those uses were for cleansing and for medicinal purposes. Yes, God can use human medicines for healing. God created this world with all of its plants, and that is precisely where we get our medicines.

As the old hymn says,

> This is my Father's world, and to my list'ning ears,
> All nature sings, and 'round me rings
> The music of the spheres.
> This is my Father's world: I rest me in the thought
> Of rocks and trees, of skies and seas;
> His hand the wonders wrought.

God has wrought wonderful things out of the plants. It is His creation, and he has designed it in such a way that the plants provide us with healing. Some of us take medicine for pain. Some of us take mental health medications. Some of us take medicine for chronic illnesses. God created the plants that provide the substance for these medicines. And in Bible times, one of the core medicines was olive oil.

Now, some scholars say it is possible they used the oil for medicine, but it is also possible that the oil was used more as a religious ritual. The Roman Catholic Church has a sacrament for this called Extreme Unction. This is actually one of the church's 7 Sacraments. And it comes from this passage right here in James.

If someone is sick, the priest comes to the person and anoints them with oil in the name of Jesus. And it is a perfectly sensible thing to do based on this passage in James. And in some Protestant churches, but certainly not all, the leaders are prepared to come to you and pray over you and anoint you with oil. It's perfectly biblical.

What I gather from James 5:14-15 is that healing can come in the form of a combination: prayer, a purposeful visit from leaders in the church, human medicine (based on God's plants), and of course: faith.

Some theologians have mistakenly assumed that James is more concerned with works than he is with faith. But that's nonsense. James employs both to the fullest extent. Our good works *arise* out of our deep faith. We believe in God's healing *because we have faith in Him*. We believe that if the leaders of the church will pray over us and anoint us with oil, then we will be healed. Yes, we believe in the power of prayer! And we also believe in the promises of God, and in the promises of scripture.

But let us not forget two important things: 1) We all must die, and 2) God is not a genie.

In other words, there will eventually come a time when your body will expire. Only God knows when that is to occur. The Lord gives, and the Lord takes away. God gives us life, and God takes away our life. We throw ourselves at His feet, and we beg for healing when we or someone we love is ill, but we also know there comes a time in all of our lives when we will expire. Whether we are 5 years old, or 25, or

55, or 85. Life on this earth is not eternal. We *will* expire. Let's not forget that.

And let us also remember that God is not a genie. Answers to our prayers are always subject to the decisions of God. The most mature prayer a Christian can pray is precisely the prayer that Jesus prayed when he was facing death, "Father, if you are willing, take this cup from me; yet not my will, but yours be done" (Luke 22:42).

We pray for healing, but we know these two things: 1) We will die. And 2) God is not our personal genie. He has a larger plan. And, as James says earlier in his epistle, we are but a vapor, a mist (4:14). Here today, gone tomorrow. Our duty is to give thanks to God for allowing us to enjoy His precious gift of life for the years that we have the opportunity.

James then interweaves *confession* into the context of prayer and healing. We pray for forgiveness. This is crucial for the Christ follower. We confess our sins to God, and we confess our sins to each other, just as James says in 5:16, "Therefore confess your sins to each other and pray for each other so that you may be healed."

And the implications here are obvious. We must be *open and vulnerable* with each other. We must have prayer partners. We must develop close relationships with other believers, so we have accountability in our walk with Christ. We must truly *trust* each other. We must have confidential talks that take us deep into our own imperfections. We must ask that others pray for us. But we must be willing to pray faithfully for them, too.

James is here describing a very healthy church. They have solid leaders who are responsive to the needs of the congregation. They are a praying community. They believe in

God's healing. They are aware of their sins, and they are sharing their sins with each other so that they may healed of their sin as well as their physical ailments. It is a beautiful scene, the way a healthy church should function.

Let's take the book of James and help our churches become healthier. Let's be people who pray often and for everything. Let's be like the prophets of old, like Elijah, who prayed for rain. Let's live righteous lives so that our prayers will be more effective, just as James says in 5:16: "The prayer of a righteous person is powerful and effective."

James ends his book (5:19-20) with a call for the people in the church to look after each other. We all know the story of the shepherd and his 100 sheep. If one wanders off, the Good Shepherd will leave the 99 in order to bring that one sheep back into the fold. Let's you and I do that. Let's reach out to those who wander away from the flock. Let's go to them.

If we know a person who has sinned badly ... instead of humiliating them on social media, let's go to them, and try to bring them back. Let's pray with them. Let's pray for them. Let's not ridicule them for their wayward path. Rather, let's explain to them the gospel—that God freely offers His forgiveness to those who repent and come back to their senses.

Friends, that's the book of James. In the final chapter, we'll summarize the themes in the book, and bring it all back together.

Take-Homes from James 5:13-20

1. Prayer is like breathing for the Christian. All. The. Time.

2. Confession of sin, prayer, and healing are all intertwined.

3. Reach out to those who wander, and bring them back into the fold.

12. Reflecting Back on Our Study of James

Conclusion

I hope you have benefitted from the teachings of *Jakob*–James–the half-brother of Jesus. He probably understood Jesus better than any other author in the New Testament. Think about it, James probably spent good time with Jesus growing up. Eating together, going on pilgrimage as a family, losing loved ones together, attending synagogue, enjoying Shabbat each week for many years.

Naturally, Jesus would have been known best by his family. Most likely, nobody knew Jesus better than his mother, Mary. And Joseph–Jesus's father–seems to have died when Jesus was a young man, since he drops out of the story after the scene where Jesus teaches in the Temple at the age of 12. Joseph probably passed away at some point between the years of 12 and 30 for Jesus.

Jesus's siblings, obviously, would have known him very well. But we know from scripture that they had their doubts about him being the long-awaited Jewish Messiah. In John 7:1-5, we learn that Jesus's brothers and sisters doubted him.

> After this, Jesus went around in Galilee. He did not want to go about in Judea because the Jewish leaders there were looking for a way to kill him. 2 But when the Jewish Festival of Tabernacles was near, 3 Jesus' brothers said to him, "Leave Galilee and go to Judea, so that your disciples there may see the works you do. 4 No one who wants to become a public figure acts in secret. Since you are doing these things, show yourself to the world." 5 For even his own brothers did not believe in him.

However, we know from 1 Corinthians that after the resurrection, Jesus appeared to his brother James, which was clearly the turning point in James's life. After he encountered the risen Jesus, he swiftly became the leader of the early church. Here is the apostle Paul's fascinating account of Jesus's appearances, in 1 Cor. 15:3-8:

> For what I received I passed on to you as of first importance: that Christ died for our sins according to the Scriptures, 4 that he was buried, that he was raised on the third day according to the Scriptures, 5 and that he appeared to Cephas, and then to the Twelve. 6 After that, he appeared to more than five hundred of the brothers and sisters at the same time, most of whom are still living, though some have fallen asleep. 7 Then he appeared to James, then to all the apostles, 8 and last of all he appeared to me also, as to one abnormally born.

And then the next thing we know, James is the obvious leader of the early Christian movement. Paul refers to James,

Cephas (Peter), and John as the clear leaders of early Christianity. Here is what Paul writes in Galatians 2:8-10,

> For God, who was at work in Peter as an apostle to the circumcised, was also at work in me as an apostle to the Gentiles. 9 James, Cephas, and John, those esteemed as pillars, gave me and Barnabas the right hand of fellowship when they recognized the grace given to me. They agreed that we should go to the Gentiles, and they to the circumcised. 10 All they asked was that we should continue to remember the poor, the very thing I had been eager to do all along.

We see that James was one of the "three esteemed pillars" of the early Church.

We also see James taking a presiding role over the famous Jerusalem Council in Acts 15:12-19:

> The whole assembly became silent as they listened to Barnabas and Paul telling about the signs and wonders God had done among the Gentiles through them. 13 When they finished, James spoke up. "Brothers," he said, "listen to me. 14 Simon [Peter] has described to us how God first intervened to choose a people for his name from the Gentiles. 15 The words of the prophets are in agreement with this, as it is written:
>
> 16 "'After this I will return
>   and rebuild David's fallen tent.
> Its ruins I will rebuild,
>   and I will restore it,
> 17 that the rest of mankind may seek the Lord,

> even all the Gentiles who bear my name,
> says the Lord, who does these things
> 18   things known from long ago.'
>
> 19 It is my judgment, therefore, that we should not make it difficult for the Gentiles who are turning to God."

Scholars agree that James was probably the primary decision-maker in the early church. James was the one to whom Paul and Barnabas reported, and it was James who made the "judgment" at the Council of Jerusalem that Gentiles should be allowed into the faith. This decision from James opened the floodgates to Gentiles turning to the Lord and joining the once-very Jewish movement of Christianity.

And then once again, in Acts chapter 21, we see Paul going up to Jerusalem to report to James, to tell him about the expansion of the gospel into the Gentile world. This is from Acts 21:17-19,

> When we arrived at Jerusalem, the brothers and sisters received us warmly. 18 The next day Paul and the rest of us went to see James, and all the elders were present. 19 Paul greeted them and reported in detail what God had done among the Gentiles through his ministry.

The next historical piece of information we get about James is regarding his death, which occurred in the year A.D. 62. According to three reliable sources: Clement of Alexandria, Hegesippus, and Josephus, James was condemned to death by the scribes and Pharisees. They took him up to the top of the Jerusalem Temple, and threw him down to the ground. He was severely injured, but not dead. So they proceeded to stone him. There was a final blow from a club to ensure he was dead. During his death he cried out, "Lord God our Father, forgive them, for they know not what they do."[1]

James, the brother of Jesus, was surely a great man. He was martyred for Christ. His life and death are a testimony to us as followers of Jesus.

And we are fortunate to have this small, five-chapter letter of James in our Bibles. We don't know when James wrote his epistle, but scholars say it is probably the earliest book of the entire New Testament, giving it a wonderful authenticity that is obvious upon reading it. Most scholars date the book of James to around A.D. 45, just a decade or so after the resurrection of Jesus. It is a very early book, written in the early years of the Christian faith. It is an important book for the church today. We need to be more familiar with it.

James has wonderful wisdom for us. Let's review what we have learned:

First, in James chapter 1, he tells us that we are going to have many trials and temptations, but we must be joyful in that suffering because God is transforming us throughout the process. We are being molded and shaped when we go through those difficult times.

James then tells us we must have strong faith in God when we pray. We must not pray weak prayers. We must pray with confidence that God will come to us, hear us, and answer our prayers.

---

[1] Amanda Kolson Hurley, "The Last Days of James," *BAS (Biblical Archaeology Society) Library*, November/December 2002, https://www.baslibrary.org/biblical-archaeology-review/28/6/14?ip_login_no_cache=%93A%3E%FF%FE%5E%97%85.

James reminds us that our lives are like flowers. We bloom for a very short time, then we pass away. He says we must not take pride in our wealth because of this vapor-like existence we have on this earth. We are here today, and gone tomorrow. Thus, we must not hoard our wealth. Our riches pale in comparison with the "crown of life that the Lord has promised to those who love Him" (James 1:12).

James warns us to watch out for our temper. He commands us to be "... slow to speak, and slow to become angry" (James 1:19). We must be very careful with our anger. Instead, we must humble ourselves when in the presence of others.

James famously tells us that we must not just listen to the Word of God. Rather, we are commanded to "Do what it says" (James 1:22). This is the main point of James. Faith in Jesus without obedience is dead faith. Let us have living faith, James urges us. Faith is exhibited in our obedience.

In the second chapter, James returns to the topic of rich people. He warns us that we must be very careful when it comes to riches. And when it comes to trying to impress rich people, we must not show favoritism. God has "... chosen those who are poor in the eyes of the world to be rich in faith and to inherit the kingdom he promised to those who love him" (James 2:5).

Then James launches into his main thesis in the second chapter. He tells us very plainly that "... faith by itself, if it is not accompanied by action, is dead" (James 2:17). Christianity is not about good intentions. It is about *doing* good. Good intentions without the good actions are empty. James makes that crystal clear.

Again, in chapter 2, verse 20, James says, "... faith without deeds is useless."

In James chapter 3, we are hit with that wonderful section on "taming the tongue." James tells us that our tongue is "a restless evil, full of deadly poison" (James 3:8). We can tame all kinds of animals, but many of us struggle to tame our tongue. Our words demonstrate the contents of our heart. We must always strive to conquer the tongue so that we have it under the control of Jesus Christ.

Also in chapter 3, James warns us against having bitterness, envy, and selfishness in our hearts. These problems are demonic, he says. These kinds of qualities tear people apart, and lead to chaos in your life.

We must be peace-loving, impartial, and sincere with people. We must be submissive to others, and full of mercy in our dealings with people. We must always be on a path to purify our hearts. Jesus was the Prince of Peace, and Christians should excel in this quality. Let us never allow disorder, chaos, and bitterness to get into our lives. And let us never allow these qualities to enter our churches. We must be vigilant to help each other through those times when we get bitter, angry, or selfish. We need the church. And we need members of the church to keep us all accountable.

In chapter four, James continues to remind us that "God opposes the proud, but shows favor to the humble" (James 4:6).

He then implores us to "Resist the devil" and "Come near to God" (James 4:7-8).

In very bold language, James tells us that we should "... not slander one another," and we must not "speak against a brother or a sister" in the church (James 4:11). Judging other Christians is forbidden. We must not do it. Jesus also hits that point very hard in his own ministry.

Chapter four ends with James reminding us that we are "mist that appears for a little while and then vanishes"

(James 4:14). Therefore, we must remain humble and avoid boasting about the future.

In the final chapter of James, we are warned about the dangers of money. Hoarding is a sin. We must pay our employees fairly. We must be generous with people who work for us.

James reminds us that we should "stand firm" in our faith. We must be patient in our suffering, like Job was.

Finally, James tells us that we need to be praying for each other. We should have faith that God will answer our prayers. He will heal us when we pray for one another. Praying to God is effective!

This wonderful epistle ends with James telling us that if anybody wanders away from the faith, then we should go get them, and lead them back to the flock.

I hope we all try to do this. If you know someone who has wandered away from their church family, then go after them. Let them know they have a family that is waiting for them to come back home.

Take-Homes from James

- Select your favorite passage from this amazing book of the Bible. Write it down. Email to your friends. Post it on your Instagram!

- "Do what it says" at some place in your life where you have been failing to do so.

- "Do what it says" is the thesis of James's epistle. Let us be "quick to listen" to his exhortation.

About the Author

If you feel generous and have a couple of minutes, please leave a review where you purchased the book if online. Thank you in advance.

Dyron B. Daughrity is the William S. Banowsky Chair in Religion at Pepperdine University in Malibu, California. He is the author of many books and articles in the fields of comparative religion, global Christianity, and world religious history. He has ministered to churches for over 30 years, and is currently the Senior Minister at the Hilltop Community Church of Christ in El Segundo, California. Dyron has been married to Sunde for 28 years and they have four children.

Visit Dyron Daughrity's website at
https://seaver.pepperdine.edu/academics/faculty/dyron-daughrity/

Visit his Amazon Author page at
https://www.amazon.com/stores/Dyron-B.-Daughrity/author/B001JS3L2G

About the Publisher

Sulis International Press publishes select fiction and non-fiction in a variety of genres under four imprints: Riversong Books, Sulis Academic Press, Sulis Press, and Keledei Publications.

For more, visit the website at
https://sulisinternational.com

Subscribe to the newsletter at
https://sulisinternational.com/subscribe/

Follow us on social media
https://www.facebook.com/SulisInternational
https://twitter.com/Sulis_Intl
https://www.pinterest.com/Sulis_Intl/
https://www.instagram.com/sulis_international/

www.ingramcontent.com/pod-product-compliance
Lightning Source LLC
Chambersburg PA
CBHW032127090426
42743CB00007B/505